Living

by

FAITH

Wallace H. Heflin, Jr.

LIVING BY FAITH

All biblical quotations are from the Authorized King James Version of the Bible.

McDougal Publishing is a ministry of The McDougal Foundation, Inc., a Maryland nonprofit corporation dedicated to spreading the Gospel of the Lord Jesus Christ to as many people as possible in the shortest time possible.

Published by:

McDougal Publishing
P.O. Box 3595
Hagerstown, MD 21742-3595

ISBN 13: 978-1-58158-113-3

Printed in the United States of America
For worldwide distribution

Contents

Foreword by Jane Lowder

"When I heard Jimmie Lee, my sister-in-law, say, 'Yes, she's here,' I knew that something was wrong. It was after midnight, and no one would be calling me that time of the night otherwise.

"It was Debbie Slayton, and I couldn't believe what she was telling me. Brother Heflin had suffered a massive heart attack coming home from a visit to a funeral home, and he had never recovered consciousness. He was gone.

"The moment was surreal. I was sure that what she was saying could not possibly be true, but I was also sure that she would not call me if something had not happened.

" 'It cant be!' I insisted.

" 'But it is!' she answered.

" 'It just can't be!' I said again.

" 'But it is!' she repeated. 'It's the truth. He's gone.'

"The news was particularly devastating to me because of the timing. We had lost our mother in February of that year, and now I had lost my spiritual father and mentor as well.

"Soon after Debbie and I hung up, I began to make arrangements to fly back to the camp the next day, but even as I did, my mind was in a turmoil. 'Why?' my mind shouted. 'Why would this happen?' I was afraid to voice the question to God. He always did things well, but His reasons were surely hidden to me this time. I couldn't imagine why this would happen. We expected Brother Heflin to outlive us all.

"My mind rushed back over the past few weeks. I had gone with Brother Heflin and a small group to Brazil, and there we had witnessed amazing signs and wonders. Many Brazilians had been healed and set free as he laid his hands on them and prayed. He had insisted that I minister every night, but I thought this was just his kind way of giving me an opportunity. I never dreamed that he was getting us ready for the days ahead—when he would no longer be with us.

"Because there had been just a few of us in the team, I had been able to speak more with him in a few days than I had over many years, and we had talked of many things concerning the future of the camp. He had been excited about the future and did not seem to be making plans to leave us. He had a lot to live for. Things were going very well for him and his ministry worldwide.

"He had seemed to have a very bad cold during those days, but none of us had considered it to be anything life-threatening. This was a man who didn't let anything keep him down, and yet now he was gone. He was dead. What would happen to the camp ministry? What would happen to all of us?

"Because it involved a death, the airlines gave me no problem about changing my ticket, but I then encountered a series of flight delays and changes throughout the day. Atlanta was fogged in, so my flight was late leaving for there. Then, when I did get into Atlanta, I couldn't get out. In the end, I was not able to fly into Richmond at all. I had to be rerouted to Dulles Airport near Washington, D.C., and I had to call for someone to pick me up there. It took me sixteen hours to get home.

"During those hours getting back to camp, I was not feeling very good about what I would find once I got there. Who would be there? What changes faced us in the days ahead? Was there anyone who could pick up the pieces and keep us moving forward? The camp team was made up of people of such distinct personalities. Brother Heflin had been strong enough to pull us all together, but could we work well together in his absence? I wasn't sure that we could.

"As I contemplated all of this, a song began to work its way into my spirit: 'I will arise and go forth in the name of the Lord of Hosts, for He has conquered every foe, by His name, by His name.' I wept as these powerful words went over and over in my spirit, and I began to feel strength coming into my mind, my spirit and my body.

"What I would face when I got back I still wasn't sure, but I knew that every foe had been conquered—even death. The death of our leader would not be allowed to bring a halt to the great ministry of the camp.

"And the other foe—the fear of what our continued living might mean—was conquered during those hours as well. My mind still couldn't comprehend how we could go forward without Brother Heflin, but my spirit was at peace about the prospect."

Jane Lowder
High and Lifted Up
(Hagerstown, Maryland.
McDougal Publishing: 2001)

What doth it profit, my brethren, though a man say he hath faith, and have not works? can faith save him? If a brother or sister be naked, and destitute of daily food, and one of you say unto them, Depart in peace, be ye warmed and filled; notwithstanding ye give them not those things which are needful to the body; what doth it profit? Even so faith, if it hath not works, is dead, being alone.

Yea, a man may say, Thou hast faith, and I have works: show me thy faith without thy works, and I will show thee my faith by my works. Thou believest that there is one God; thou doest well: the devils also believe, and tremble.

But wilt thou know, O vain man, that faith without works is dead? Was not Abraham our father justified by works, when he had offered Isaac his son upon the altar? Seest thou how faith wrought with his works, and by works was faith made perfect? And the scripture was fulfilled which saith, Abraham believed God, and it was imputed unto him for righteousness: and he was called the Friend of God. Ye see then how that by works a man is justified, and not by faith only.

Likewise also was not Rahab the harlot jus-tified by works, when she had received the messengers, and had sent them out another way? For as the body without the spirit is dead, so faith without works is dead also.

James 2:14-26

Introduction

There has never been a time in the history of the Church when faith was preached more than it is today, and yet we see so little display of it. Much is being *said*, but very little is being *done*. This is contrary to the biblical concept of faith. Real faith, the Bible shows us, always produces something. So we need less talk and more action, less profession of faith and more performance of faith. Faith is not talking, but living.

I am blessed to have a great heritage of faith. Our parents not only taught us faith; they lived faith before us. They came into Pentecost at an important time, a time in which people of faith depended on God for everything and were not ashamed of or afraid to declare that fact to others. Indeed they were proud to do so, and they didn't fear what men might think or say about them. Because of that, they experienced amazing miracles. I owe my parents a great debt of gratitude, for from them I learned the simple concepts that have allowed me to believe God to see His hand move in my life consistently over a period of many years.

I'm not at all sure that I can define faith, for faith

can neither be fully understood nor fully explained. It's something you must experience. And when you have faith, sometimes you don't know how you know that something is true; you just know it. Faith is a miracle of God, a miracle that enables us to tap into the vast resources of Heaven.

My father was a preacher of faith. Whatever text he chose from the Bible, he ended up preaching about faith, for he had learned that faith is the key that unlocks all the mysteries of God, and that if we can only believe, all things become possible to us.

But, again, he was not just a preacher of faith; he lived a life of faith. That was the greatest legacy he could have left us, for the very best way to demonstrate faith is by example.

Because of the example set for us by my parents, I'm constantly challenged to greater faith, and I'm also compelled to challenge those whom I meet everywhere to stop talking and to start doing, to stop trying to understand faith and to start practicing it. For, as Jesus said: *"all things are possible to him that believeth"* (Mark 9:23). Now, through the pages of this book, I hope to challenge *you* to have faith in God, to have an ever-increasing faith, and to learn what it means to begin *LIVING BY FAITH.*

Wallace H. Heflin, Jr.
1996

Part I

The Need for Faith

Chapter 1

The Value of Faith

But without faith it is impossible to please him: for he that cometh to God must believe that he is, and that he is a rewarder of them that diligently seek him.   Hebrews 11:6

Your faith is the most important thing you possess. Faith pleases God, and *"without faith it is impossible to please him."* Therefore, if you have been taught faith, you're one of the most blessed people who have ever lived.

Faith Moves God

Tears don't always move God, but faith always does. Our sacrifices don't always move Him, but faith always does. A broken heart doesn't always move Him, but faith always does. Need doesn't always move Him, but faith always does.

God is not necessarily moved by the lack of food

in your cupboards or by the lack of fuel for your stove, but if your faith is strong, there will always be enough food in your cupboards and enough fuel for your stove. Faith always moves the hand of God. It always causes Him to intervene in the affairs of men and to work on their behalf. Therefore, we all need faith, and we all need more faith.

Faith (or a Lack of Faith) Is the Only Thing Hindering You

Your level of faith is the only thing hindering you. There are no other limitations in God. *"All things are possible,"* but to whom? *"To him that believeth."*

Many of the people who come to our camp tell me that they have never before been challenged to do something for God. No one has ever told them that *they* can travel for the Lord—to Israel, to China, to Russia, or to any other nation. No one has ever told them that *they* can lay hands on the sick and expect to see miracles of healing. No one has ever told them that *they* can cast out demons and see men and women set free.

When they receive a word from the Lord and someone lays hands on them, so that the vision of the Lord becomes real and understood in their lives, suddenly their faith soars. They may not have any money at the time, but they begin to rejoice because they know that God is working for *them* and that *they* will soon be launched forth in a new way.

How those same people rejoice when they eventually stand on foreign soil proclaiming the goodness of the Lord! They know that God has done the work and that they're there in that foreign land preaching the Gospel because of faith in God and no other reason.

God is ready to do the same miracle for all those who will dare to believe Him. Nothing is impossible—to him that believeth.

Faith Produces Miracles

Once, when it was nearly time to leave with a group for the Holy Land, a lady called me early in the morning and asked if she could go. "We're leaving this evening," I told her.

"I know, Brother Heflin," she said. "I sent in my two-hundred-dollar deposit, but only this morning my husband agreed to put the rest of the trip on his American Express card."

I wasn't surprised. God is famous for His last-minute rescues. That woman was with us when

17

we boarded our transatlantic flight in New York that same evening.

Another lady, a friend of the first, when she heard that her friend was able to go, also called me, at nine in the morning that same day. "Brother Heflin," she said, "I simply must go with you."

"Do you know that we're leaving this evening?" I asked.

"Yes, I know," she replied.

"Then why didn't you call me last week?" I asked.

"Can I go?" she countered.

"I don't know if we can work out all the details," I told her. "I'll call you later after I've talked with the agents and let you know if it's possible."

At ten o'clock she called to say that her daughter wanted to go too and to ask if it would be possible. From noon of the previous day until time to leave that evening, eleven more people were added to our group. God had given them all a last-minute miracle, and we were able to get them all on the plane to Israel.

The airlines had wanted their payment twenty-one days before departure and had put heavy pressure on the agents, threatening to cancel any tickets that were not paid by that time. But, thank God, He had other ideas. He helps us at the last minute, when we trust Him.

Cherish Your Faith

Faith is alive and will enable the person who exercises it to do impossible things. Therefore cherish your faith. Recognize its value. Then, protect it and hold on to it at all costs.

The value of faith and the need to nurture it and protect it was one of the themes of Paul's letter to the Galatian Christians. Some of them were guilty of not appreciating what they had in Christ and of carelessly allowing it to diminish and fail. He called them *"foolish"* because of it:

> *O foolish Galatians, who hath bewitched you, that ye should not obey the truth, before whose eyes Jesus Christ hath been evidently set forth, crucified among you? This only would I learn of you, Received ye the Spirit by the works of the law, or by the hearing of faith? Are ye so foolish? having begun in the Spirit, are ye now made perfect by the flesh?*
> Galatians 3:1-3

Paul found it hard to believe that after the Galatian Christians had received such a glorious salvation experience, they had been turned aside so soon and had begun to believe something alto-

gether different. He considered that to be very
"foolish."

There are many *"foolish"* Christians alive today.
They get hung up on all sorts of new doctrines and
ideas and try to use them to make their way fur-
ther into the Kingdom, and, in the process, they
neglect and even allow to decline that most precious possession—their faith. The result is that
they, like the Galatians, then slip back into some
of their former ways (from which they were delivered) and get drawn back into the enemy's web.

It's one thing for a person who has never had
faith to wonder if it has any value, but it's quite
another thing for a person who has known faith in
God to willingly give it up and turn back. I, too,
find that to be inconceivable. The Scriptures declare that it's like a dog returning to its vomit:

> *As a dog returneth to his vomit, so a fool
> returneth to his folly.*   Proverbs 26:11

There was great rejoicing all over the world
when the Berlin Wall came down and, one by one,
the old regimes fell in most Communist countries.
Now, years later, the people of those countries, as
a whole, would never think of returning to the
past. They're free. They can make their own deci-

sions in life. They would never go back. It's simply inconceivable to them.

To me, there's nothing worse than dead believers. They should know better. They should be farther along the road. They should have more than they do. Their faith should be rising, and they should be producing fruit for the Kingdom. Instead, they've turned back to the emptiness of the world.

This has nothing to do with prosperity, for we should be able to prosper and still maintain our faith in God. Nothing must be allowed to hinder our relationship with Him.

Don't Let *Your* Faith Be *"in Vain"*

The Galatians had paid a price for their faith. Was that price now to be *"in vain"*?

> *Have ye suffered so many things in vain?*
> Galatians 3:4

Some years ago, Mary Decker was the favored runner in the Olympics, and no one else was thought to have a chance of defeating her. But when the fateful day came, Mary tripped and fell and lost the race. If the devil can get us to trip in

21

an important moment, he can do us much harm and steal from us the prize for which we have worked so hard. We must not allow him to do that.

The great thief, who has come, Jesus said, *"to steal, and to kill, and to destroy"* (John 10:10), must not be allowed to steal our faith, kill our faith, or destroy our faith. It's far too valuable to let that happen.

The enemy of our souls is subtle. If he can't destroy us with a frontal assault, he'll employ more subtle tactics. With the Galatians, it was an attempt to get them to rely on the flesh, good works, and on obedience to the Law for salvation. Paul was forced to say to them:

> *He therefore that ministereth to you the Spirit, and worketh miracles among you, doeth he it by the works of the law, or by the hearing of faith? Even as Abraham believed God, and it was accounted to him for righteousness. Know ye therefore that they which are of faith, the same are the children of Abraham.*   Galatians 3:5-7

God's people will be made up of "[those] *which are of faith."* Therefore, this is not a time for turning back or turning aside. It's a time for going forward in faith, nurturing and protecting that precious element that God has so graciously permitted us to experience.

Never Stop Demonstrating Faith

In the early years of the Pentecostal movement in our country, Pentecostal pastors always prayed for those who were sick, and a great majority of those who were prayed for were healed. This, more than anything else, made the Pentecostal movement successful, not only here, but around the world. In recent years, however, as believers have stopped fasting and praying and stopped exercising faith and contending for healing miracles, such miracles have become a rather rare occurrence in many churches. Many pastors, therefore, no longer even pray for the sick.

A well-known Pentecostal evangelist came to our city [Richmond, Virginia] for a week of meetings, and never once, during that time, did he pray for the sick. Yet healing was one of the signs Jesus promised would follow *"them that believe"*:

> *And these signs shall follow them that believe; In my name shall they cast out devils; they shall speak with new tongues; they*

23

shall take up serpents; and if they drink any deadly thing, it shall not hurt them; THEY SHALL LAY HANDS ON THE SICK, AND THEY SHALL RECOVER. Mark 16:17-18

It's a tragedy to abandon practices that were meant to demonstrate faith to the world and thus win the world to Christ. We must not go backward in faith; we must go forward. Paul concluded:

For as many as are of the works of the law are under the curse: for it is written, Cursed is every one that continueth not in all things which are written in the book of the law to do them. But that no man is justified by the law in the sight of God, it is evident: for, THE JUST SHALL LIVE BY FAITH.

Galatians 3:10-11

There is no other way to be *"just."* There is no other way to *"please"* God. There is no other way to become *"children of Abraham."* Don't be like the *"foolish"* Galatians. Don't allow the enemy to force you back into bondage. Let your faith be released. Let it soar. Let it flourish. It's time to start *LIVING BY FAITH.* ⤵

Chapter 2

What Faith Can Do

*And ALL THINGS, whatsoever ye shall ask
in prayer, believing, ye shall receive.*

Matthew 21:22

*Jesus said unto him, If thou canst believe,
ALL THINGS are possible to him that
believeth.* Mark 9:23

What can faith do? *"All things!"*

Faith Can Produce Missing Keys

When Mother went with me one year to Haiti,
she left the key for her suitcase at home. Every
morning, for several days, my niece Edith Ann
Dowds knocked on my hotel room door asking if
Grandma could use my key to open her suitcase.
Another sister who was with us had also left her

key at home, and since my key fit both their suit-
cases, one or the other of them was always looking
for me to get the key.

Then Mother got to praying and asked God to
help her. She said, "Lord, You can bring those keys
from home and put them where I can find them,"
and that's exactly what God did. She found her two
keys fastened together with a safety pin, just as
she had left them at home. She gave one of the
keys to the other sister, and we all had keys. If you
can believe Him, God can do anything at all.

Faith Can Shorten Traveling Time

When Pastor Bell of Tabor City, North Carolina,
died, a couple carloads of us went down to his
funeral. When we were almost there, one of the
vehicles broke down. Pastor Bell's son had it
towed to a garage he was familiar with to get it
worked on while the funeral was going on.

When the funeral was over, we went to the garage to get the car. It wasn't quite finished yet, so
we left for Richmond, and others stayed behind to
come in the other car about twenty minutes later.

It was 6:20 P.M. when we left Tabor City. We had
talked to my sister Ruth, who had just arrived
home from Israel, and said to her, "It will probably

be nine o'clock before we can get back home. Go ahead and start the service [in the Richmond church], and we'll come as quickly as we can."

We had a hundred and twenty miles to go, and I wasn't in a big hurry because I knew she had things under control. When we stopped in Emporia for about ten minutes to get a bite to eat, I said to the others, "It's funny, but I don't remember passing Roanoke Rapids." And that exit is a busy place full of activity. It's not easy to miss, and yet I couldn't remember passing through it.

I drove as far as Petersburg and then Edith Ann took over. The speed limit had been lowered to 55 mph, and she would not exceed it. In fact, she was doing 54 3/4 mph all the way to Richmond.

Yet when we pulled up in front of the Richmond church, it was just seven minutes past eight o'clock. Only an hour and forty-seven minutes had gone by, not enough time to travel that far. When we got to the door, Ruth was saying, "Let's all stand as we begin our service tonight."

The second car didn't get to Richmond until nine o'clock that night, although those who rode in it left shortly after we did. What happened? I believe that the Holy Ghost picked us up and moved us over much of that territory. Faith works, and it will perform the impossible.

Faith Can Replace Defective Kneecaps and Missing Kidneys

How is it possible when surgeons have removed a man's kneecap and he no longer has normal movement in that knee that when we lay hands on him, his knee is restored and he can move it as before? I don't know, but I've had it happen to people I've prayed for. And if a kidney has been removed, God can put a new one in its place.

We prayed for a small girl in North Carolina. She was due for surgery in the next few days because she couldn't hear. But when we laid hands on her, God restored her hearing and she didn't need the operation. I don't understand it completely. What I do understand is that God said that when we lay hands on the sick, *"they shall recover."*

I don't know how He does it, and I don't want to waste my time asking Him about it, but I know it works. When I believe for it, God does it. That's enough for me. And if you, too, become foolish enough to believe Him for miracles, He will do them for you as well.

Faith Can Purchase a New Organ

Many years ago we needed a new organ for the church in Richmond. There was no money, but I felt led to go look at organs and get some prices. Seven years earlier I had bought an old Baldwin organ for $200.00, and I got a lot of good use out of it in the ministry. Now, seven years later, I asked the dealer if he could take my old Baldwin organ as a trade on a new one. When I called him back to tell him the model number, he said he would allow me $624.00 for that old organ against the new one. And it was done. That's the way God works when you start moving in faith.

What can faith do? *"All things."* Try it, and you'll see that it works.

Dead Faith Produces Nothing

But to produce something, faith must be living and vibrant. Otherwise, it's *"in vain"*—useless.

Years ago a preacher came to our camp in Ashland, Virginia, and brought with him a builder. The preacher said to my father, "Brother Heflin, would you mind if I show this contractor around the camp?"

29

Dad said, "Of course not. Just help yourself. Make yourself at home. Look at all you want to see."

The man said, "God has spoken to me, and I'm going to build a camp just like this one."

"That's wonderful," Dad said. "Just be sure you've got the faith."

"Oh, I've got the faith, all right," he answered, "and I've got the contractor right here who'll help me do it."

Dad smiled and repeated, "Just be sure you've got the faith."

Well, that was many years ago, and the first stone has yet to be turned to get that particular campmeeting going because that man's faith was not living. It was only words. He was sure he had faith, but there were never any works to add to his faith, so it didn't profit anyone. It's time for more than mere words. It's time to start *LIVING BY FAITH*.

Part II

Lessons in Faith from Moses

Chapter 3

Refusing Faith

By faith Moses, when he was come to years, REFUSED to be called the son of Pharaoh's daughter.   Hebrews 11:24

When Moses was plucked from the bulrushes, Pharaoh's daughter became his legal mother. And, although Moses was nursed by his birth mother, he was raised in Pharaoh's court. Most would have considered that to be a great stroke of luck, for the pharaohs were extremely rich and powerful people.

Moses' Amazing Choice

Nevertheless when Moses was grown, he decided that his life would not be lived in ease in the palaces of the pharaohs, but rather in service to his enslaved people, in bringing them liberty and taking them back to their own land. What was that all about? It was a decision of faith.

I'm struck by the unusual way in which God moved in this case. The pharaohs, who later continually hardened their hearts and refused to let the people of Israel go, and, in fact, were instrumental in making their life even more unbearable, raised in their own courts the man God would use to get the job done. How amazing is that?

It must have been difficult for Moses' mother to see her son living under the influence of the Egyptian royal family, but she had faith that the God who had kept them until that moment for a divine purpose would protect her son from all evil influence and that the faith she had instilled in her child would take hold and prosper in the harshest imaginable conditions. And her faith was honored.

We don't know exactly how old Moses was when the ties with his mother, as a nurse, were broken. I can imagine that in later years she often sought any and every excuse to go see him. Just as Hannah brought a coat yearly to Samuel in the Temple, I imagine that Moses' mother would make whatever small object she was able to put together and take it to her son. God had given her a way to put her foot in the door of the palace, and I believe she took advantage of it every possible way she could in the intervening years. She became Moses' mentor in every respect.

Dependent Upon the Wealth of Egypt

Until the moment Moses made that fateful decision, he was dependent upon the wealth of Egypt. He could have anything his heart desired. He could go where he wanted and eat what he wanted, and countless servants were at his beck and call at all times. But there came a day when he was forced to renounce all that. He had to make a decision not to depend upon the natural provision available to him, but rather to draw on a much greater Source. By rejecting Egypt, Moses became totally dependent upon God.

Some of you who are reading this book have been called by the Master of the Harvest to labor in His fields, but you have been afraid to let go of the security of your position and your regular income to do it. Let your faith be built up until you know that God will never fail you. He'll never let you down. So throw yourself upon the mercies of the Lord, saying, "God, I have no one but You." This will delight the heart of God, and He will prove to you that He's the very best paymaster and that He can do for you what no one else can.

Making Good Money in the World

All the years I was running from God before I was saved, I made good money, but I could never think of going overseas or of taking some exotic vacation. I always spent more than I earned, like most everyone else. But then I changed employers and moved into God's establishment, and I found that He has offices all over the world, that He's always open for business, and that He's not too big to be concerned about my personal need. Since then, He has sent me to more than eighty nations of the world on assignment for Him, and it's been a wonderfully rewarding experience.

God's central offices are located far from this earth, and someday I will be transferred there. What a wonderful boss He is! There could be no better. It's wonderful to be dependent upon Him, and exciting to see how He works in our daily lives.

Learning Not to Trust in Stocks

By the time I got saved, I had accumulated a few

hundred dollars worth of stock in the company I worked for, and I was sure that the company would continue to prosper. So, I looked forward to receiving regular dividends. Since I had no other source of income at the time, I put my faith in the future of those stocks.

One day my sister Ruth said to me, "God will never begin to provide your needs until you get rid of your stocks and stop trusting that company's profits instead of trusting Him." Today, many years later, I know that God will let us have as many stocks and bonds as we can handle, but my problem was that I had more confidence in those shares than I had in God Himself. Therefore I was determined to hold on to them—no matter what.

Eventually, however, God let me get into a financial bind that required that I sell my precious shares, and they sold very quickly. Then God began to show me that He was able to provide my every need. The Scriptures teach:

> *Thus saith the* Lord; *Cursed be the man that trusteth in man, and maketh flesh his arm, and whose heart departeth from the* Lord.   Jeremiah 17:5

37

The arm of flesh will fail you, but Jesus never will. This doesn't mean that you have to sell all your stocks and bonds. God will even give you more than you already have. You can keep them—as long as you're not dependent upon them rather than upon the goodness of the Lord.

Who's Your Source?

Realize who your Source is. If you have a good job, and you've been receiving a regular paycheck every week for many years, it's easy to become too dependent upon that paycheck and not trust God. But a job can be lost. Companies, even the largest ones, can go bankrupt. It happens every day. Learn to depend upon God. Make Him your Source for everything. If you do that, you can never go wrong. As you make the shift from trusting man to trusting God, you'll see His hand revealed. He will provide for you in unusual ways.

Mother always taught us, "Hold lightly the things of this world, and if God takes them, you won't lose your arm." If you say, "This is mine, I will never let it go," the Lord will show you that He is indeed Lord by requiring of you the thing you said you would never give up. You want to keep all the best for yourself, but God wants you to offer all the best to Him. When you do offer everything to Him, He lets you keep the best things, and when you don't offer everything to Him, He demands from you whatever He wants. The choice is yours.

Why not say to God today, "Here's my house, my car, my stocks and bonds, and my bank account; here's all that I own in this life, and it's all Yours"? Then He'll let you keep it all. If God knows that you'll be a good steward, He'll put His blessing upon all that you have, and it will prosper. Our God can provide—when He sees faith in us.

A Worthy Example

Dr. and Mrs. Jerry Kirchner sold their dental practice of twenty-six years to work for God. They were very generous with the money they derived from the sale, and God has blessed them and taken them all over the world. They travel more than anyone else associated with our Ashland Camp ministry. I was very excited one day when I received a thousand-dollar check earmarked for their ministry. A few days later, I got another check, this one from overseas. The accompanying letter simply said, "Please deposit this in Dr. Jerry's account."

God is so faithful. When you take Him as your Source, you'll do well. You'll never have to go on welfare or beg for your income. I firmly believe that if you're worth $25,000.00 a year in a secular position, you're worth more than that to God. If you're worth $50,000.00 to a secular company, you're worth more than that to God.

There's no greater provider than He. What a provider He is! Trust Him and let Him be your Source.

Faith to Build

When we needed permission to build one of our camp buildings, for the first time we had to go before the local zoning board. New laws had taken effect, and because we were in an agricultural area, we had to have a special permit to operate a church camp. They asked us to appear before the County Board of Supervisors, and there we were asked if we planned to build more in the future.

"We will build as the Lord provides," I answered.

I could see the wheels turning in their minds.

They were thinking of the way their own churches had built in the past. Most churches take ten to fifteen years to get their funds together and six months or more to get their plans together before they can even think of building. These men were thinking: "These poor Pentecostals, they'll never get their money together to expand." And that day approval was granted for our project.

In the ensuing months and years, however, we were going back to them again and again to request permission to build still another building, and the members of the commission were amazed that we could do so much. When you depend upon God, you take off all financial limits, and anything becomes possible.

We never once had the money in our hands before we began to build. Rather, we began to build because we had heard the voice of God. When you take a step to begin to do what He has spoken, He will open doors that were previously closed and make a way where there formerly seemed to be no way.

Moses Knew a Better Source

Moses refused to be dependent upon the largesse of Pharaoh, because he knew a better

Source. There comes a time when, in faith, you must refuse something of this world in order to gain the more precious treasures of the Spirit. Before you can learn to walk with God, you must refuse to walk any other way. Before you can learn to live by faith, dependent upon His goodness, you must refuse to live any other way.

Don't accept every offer. Don't fall for every trick of the enemy. Wait for God's timing and for His plan.

Egypt Was a Type of the World

One reason Moses refused to be identified with Egypt any longer was that Egypt is a type of the world and of sin. Don't be guilty of compromising for financial gain. In actuality, you will gain nothing by doing that. God's Word is very clear on this point:

> *Wherefore come out from among them, and be ye separate, saith the Lord, and touch not the unclean thing; and I will receive you.*
> 2 Corinthians 6:17

It's time that the Church learned to do some

refusing. God has not blessed you so that you can sing in nightclubs or perform in unwholesome movies or sell sinful and harmful things to others. He forbids us to do anything that could become a stumbling block to our brothers:

> ... *that no man put a stumblingblock or an occasion to fall in his brother's way.*
>
> Romans 14:13

> *But whoso shall offend one of these little ones which believe in me, it were better for him that a millstone were hanged about his neck, and that he were drowned in the depth of the sea.* Matthew 18:6

Believers have no business in certain places doing certain things—no matter how lucrative their contracts might be. It's better to refuse and to let people know that you no longer do the things you used to do.

Don't Be Drawn into Compromise

Why is it that so many believers are drawn into compromising situations? It should be the opposite. We should be showing the world an example of what it means to live godly lives and believe our Father for our daily needs.

If you've ever walked at night behind someone with a flashlight, you know that it's possible for them to see the path and yet for you to see nothing. The secret is to ask them to raise the source of the light a little. When they raise it, that light spreads out and covers a wider area, making it possible for you to see too.

So raise your light. It's time to let the light shine in the area of finances. Jesus said:

> *Let your light so shine before men, that they may see your good works, and glorify your Father which is in heaven.*   Matthew 5:16

Let everyone see. Let them see your light. Let them see your good works. Let them see your love for God. Let them see your devotion to His cause. If you're doing the same rotten things you did before God saved you, what are men and women to think? They have every right to wonder if you are a true Christian.

Why is it that Christian musicians and singers feel they have to break into the popular music of the world in order to be successful? If you spend time in the coal bin of life, you'll come out covered with black dust. And once you become accustomed to being covered with dust, you'll no longer feel uncomfortable with it and be concerned to wash it off as quickly as possible.

Learn to Refuse the Offers of This World

Learn to refuse the offers of this world. They'll get you nowhere. Refuse to be identified with that which is not pleasing to God. Refuse to lower your standards to please others. Refuse to water down your faith.

If you want to win your loved ones to the Lord, you must refuse to lower yourself to their level of conduct, and begin setting a standard for them to aspire to. If a woman wants to win her officer husband to the Lord, she must stop going drinking with him at the officers' club. Compromise doesn't impress anyone. Have refusing faith. If you lower yourself to the standards of others, not only do you fail to win them, but you also put your own soul in jeopardy.

For forty years Moses had been known as

45

Pharaoh's grandson. One tradition is that this particular pharaoh had no son and so Moses was next in line for the throne. If so, it must have seemed to Moses like a lot to give up. Still, he didn't hesitate. He had his sights on greater treasures, heavenly treasures. And you need to lift your sights too. It's time to start *LIVING BY FAITH*.

Chapter 4

Choosing Faith

... CHOOSING rather to suffer affliction with the people of God, than to enjoy the pleasures of sin for a season.   Hebrews 11:25

Having refusing faith freed Moses to have choosing faith. Because he refused to be content with second best, he was free to make the right choices in life.

Moses Chose to Suffer

Moses chose to suffer because he understood that the afflictions of the righteous are *"for a season"* and will end in an eternity of blessing, but that the pleasures of sin are also *"for a season"* and will end in an eternity of suffering and separation from God.

Oh, it's no fun to be misunderstood by others, no

fun to be persecuted and hated, rejected and despised. But these are not reasons to turn aside from following Jesus. These sufferings are temporal—*"for a season."* It always pays to serve God, so it's a wise choice, and choosing faith makes the right choice every time.

God Doesn't Hide the Cost of Believing

God doesn't hide the cost of believing. It's very clear in His Word. The first thing Ananias was to tell Saul of Tarsus when he visited him in Damascus was how great a price he would pay for his decision to follow Christ:

> *For I will show him how great things he must suffer for my name's sake.* Acts 9:16

There *is* a fleshly suffering that accompanies service to God. There *is* a price to be paid, but Moses gladly chose it. Jesus chose it, as well:

> *Though he were a Son, yet learned he obedience by the things which he suffered.*
> Hebrews 5:8

Now God is calling upon every one of us to make the same choice in life:

And if children, then heirs; heirs of God, and joint-heirs with Christ; if so be that we suffer with him, that we may be also glorified together. Romans 8:17

If we suffer, we shall also reign with him: if we deny him, he also will deny us.
2 Timothy 2:12

When we have made a decision to serve the Lord "come what may," then nothing that we face in life can turn us aside. We're no longer affected by criticism or jealousy or disappointment in seeing the failures and weaknesses of others. Choosing faith sets us on a straight course and prevents us from detouring or ever turning back.

The afflictions we suffer as believers never harm us spiritually. In fact, each of them draws us closer to God, and they become, in this way, a blessing to us—a blessing in disguise.

Moses Knew Who He Was

Moses could choose a better way of life because

he knew who he was. Oh yes, he knew that the people around him recognized him as the son of Pharaoh's daughter, and he knew that he was probably next in line for the throne. But he also knew that he was born of parents of faith who had risked their own lives to protect him because they believed he had been born for a divine purpose. He knew that only by a miracle had he been spared the mandate of Pharaoh to kill all boy babies among the despised Hebrews. And he knew that only by a miracle was his mother able to nurse him in his younger years, and, in so doing, to teach him about the one true God.

If Moses had been willing, at that point, to renounce his mother, he could have had the throne, but he couldn't do it. "That Hebrew woman" was his true mother, and he was proud of that fact. Pharaoh's daughter had given him many things his mother could not afford to give him, but his mother had given him something that all the wealth of Egypt never could have. He was rich in God, rich in faith, and rich in heritage. He didn't need Egypt. Egypt would only hold him back. Egypt would only rob him of greatness.

Every one of us has these same choices to make in life. You might call them "hard choices," but to

Moses there wasn't anything hard about them. His choice was clear. His way was plain. Recognizing who his mother was made him recognize who he was. For he was of the same faith, and he was of the same heritage. He was made of the same stuff.

There was a price attached to this decision, and from the day Moses made it, he became a stranger and a sojourner in Egypt and had to flee for his life. But he had no complaints, for he had chosen his lot in life. You and I also need choosing faith because we have some very important decisions to make.

Joshua's Challenge Was the Same

When the Promised Land was within the grasp of the children of Israel, Joshua challenged them to make a serious choice:

> *And if it seem evil unto you to serve the LORD, choose you this day whom ye will serve; whether the gods which your fathers served that were on the other side of the flood, or the gods of the Amorites, in whose land ye dwell: but as for me and my house, we will serve the LORD.*   Joshua 24:15

Moses had demanded the same choice in his day:

> *I call heaven and earth to record this day against you, that I have set before you life and death, blessing and cursing: therefore choose life, that both thou and thy seed may live.* Deuteronomy 30:19

The decisions you make will affect not only your own life; they will also affect the lives of your family members and friends.

Know the Facts

In order to choose wisely, you must know all the facts, and the fact is that certain afflictions accompany the life of faith:

> *Yea, and all that will live godly in Christ Jesus shall suffer persecution.*
> 2 Timothy 3:12

> *Many are the afflictions of the righteous: but the LORD delivereth him out of them all.*
> Psalm 34:19

CHOOSING FAITH

There has always been a reproach connected with the Pentecostal faith, and to escape that reproach some have watered down the message, trying to make it acceptable to the majority of the community. Some stopped saying "speaking in tongues" and started saying "glossolalia." Since most people didn't understand that word, it was not considered quite as offensive.

It's true that if you water down the message enough so that it's hard to tell the difference between a Pentecostal and any other mainline denominational Christian, it does lessen the persecution. But is it worth it in the end? Wouldn't it be better to follow Moses' lead, choosing to suffer here *"for a season"* in order to rejoice with God throughout the ages of eternity? Just as there is a certain reproach that comes with serving God, there is also a unique joy that comes to you when you have made the proper decisions in life. So make them. Have choosing faith. It's time to start *Living by Faith*.

Chapter 5

Evaluating Faith

Esteeming the reproach of Christ greater riches than the treasures in Egypt: for he had respect unto the recompence of the reward.

Hebrews 11:26

Moses knew the value of his faith; it was worth more than all the riches of Egypt. And that's saying a lot. At the time Moses lived, Egypt was the dominant nation in the world, and it was a rich one indeed. Just the value of the gold-covered sarcophagi kept in the Cairo Museum represents a fantastic treasure. And yet what we have in God is worth more than all the gold in the entire world. Throw in all the silver and jewels as well, and our faith is still worth more.

"The Treasures in Egypt"

One entire room of the Cairo Museum is dedicated to treasures found in the tomb of King Tut. Aside from the gold-covered sarcophagi, there are necklaces and earrings of gold. And that is just the beginning. It is such a vast treasure that armed guards stand at the doors of that room, and other armed guards are placed strategically throughout the museum.

What would be the value of the artifacts in that one room? I doubt that anyone would dare to even try placing a value on it. We would just have to say that it's "priceless."

The pyramids of Egypt are one of the seven wonders of the world. And there are many other priceless statues and buildings among Egypt's ancient sites. So Egypt was rich beyond imagination. Still, Moses caught sight of something far more valuable.

Just as Moses, you and I are not of this world. Therefore, we must refuse to lay up treasures here, for Jesus taught us:

> *Lay not up for yourselves treasures upon earth, where moth and rust doth corrupt, and where thieves break through and steal: but lay up for yourselves treasures in heaven, where neither moth nor rust doth corrupt, and where thieves do not break*

*through nor steal: for where your treasure
is, there will your heart be also.*

Matthew 6:19-21

We have greater treasures than those that can be accumulated in bank vaults or in Wall Street stocks. We have eternal treasures.

The Riches of Heaven

One day, when we've seen Heaven's gates of pearl and streets of pure gold, we'll know that it has been worth it all to serve Jesus and that nothing in this world can compare with the treasures we've been storing up in Heaven. And it's your faith that will get you to that glorious place.

A millionaire can die and go to Hell, but faith can assure you a place at the Master's side. The poorest Christian who has believed the Gospel and invited Christ to come in and dwell will far outstrip the wealthiest man who doesn't have that particular treasure. Never look at what you might lose if you follow God. Look, instead, at what you'll surely gain.

Jesus showed us that the soul cannot have a price, or a monetary value, placed on it. He said:

For what is a man profited, if he shall gain the whole world, and lose his own soul? or what shall a man give in exchange for his soul?   Matthew 16:26

If you don't understand the value of your salvation, you may become unwilling to pay the price necessary to maintain it. This is why so many are now willingly relinquishing what God has given them. They're unable or unwilling to properly evaluate what they have. Something else seems more important or more rewarding to them at the moment.

When we value our experience, then we become willing to bear Christ's reproach:

Let us go forth therefore unto him without the camp, bearing his reproach.

Hebrews 13:13

What we suffer here is a very small price to pay when we think of what awaits us in eternity.

Yes, There Are Pleasures in Sin

We cannot deny that there are definite *"plea-*

sures" associated with the sins of the flesh. Everyone knows that. If there were no pleasures in sin, no one would be drawn to it. The devil surely knows about those pleasures, for if they didn't exist, he would be powerless to tempt men to sin. But you can only buy joy *"for a season."* When I was a sinner, I bought all that I could afford and more, but it never lasted nearly long enough to suit me.

It's no mystery why everyone wants to live beyond his or her means. It's an attempt to buy joy and happiness. And yet the Lord says to us:

> *Ho, every one that thirsteth, come ye to the waters, and he that hath no money; come ye, buy, and eat; yea, come, buy wine and milk without money and without price.* Isaiah 55:1

The happiness which the Lord gives is not only eternal; it also has no strings attached. Worldly pleasure, on the other hand, is not only temporary; it also ties you at every opportunity. Moses understood this and made the wise choice. He had evaluating faith.

Pleasure vs. Affliction

Pleasure is better than affliction any day. Or is it? In the case of Moses, pleasure and affliction represented two very different roads. One led upward, and the other led downward.

We often have a false sense that people around us are looking down on us because of our stand for Christ, but that's impossible. You're moving ever upward, and they're on a downward course. So it's impossible for them to look down on you.

If you've chosen the upward way, put your shoulders back, hold your head high, and say, "Devil, you're a liar. I've chosen the right way. I've chosen the heavenly vision. I've chosen to follow Jesus."

We're not walking this way because it's the way indicated by our particular denomination. We're walking this way because of personal choice to live a life pleasing to God. It's a result of evaluating faith.

Refuse to Believe the Enemy's Lies

When the enemy tries to make you feel that your life has no value and that your choice was a wrong one, just stop and take a good look around you. Take a good look at the fruit of the lives of those who have chosen the high road, and take an equally good look at the fruit of the lives of the compromisers, and you'll again be set on the proper course in life. Always take the high road.

Choose not to be a compromiser. Choose not to lower your standards. Choose to live as the Lord directs you. Evaluating faith will enable you to make these proper choices.

Don't ever be ashamed of who you are in Christ and of what you have in Him. Make a firm choice based on a proper evaluation and then stand upon it, and you'll never be sorry.

Yes, there are temporary pleasures in sin, but the ultimate payment, *"the wages of sin,"* is not pleasant in any sense. Paul wrote to the Romans:

> *For the wages of sin is death; but the gift of God is eternal life through Jesus Christ our Lord.* Romans 6:23

Moses knew this thousands of years before Paul wrote it, and based on his knowledge, he made a proper evaluation. He was not willing to live for the moment, and he was not willing to live for the day. He chose to live for the future, realizing that what we do today affects all our tomorrows. He had an eye for eternity.

Strangely enough, when Moses made his decision to abandon Egypt, he had not yet experienced the burning bush, and he had never been privileged to sit at the feet of a Jewish rabbi in synagogue. He was still living in the courts of Pharaoh, but God was dealing with his heart.

What Causes Us to Sacrifice for God?

Why would a man leave his business and go out to serve God? Why would a man leave his country and go to some strange place to serve God? We can only say that the man or woman who does it has made a wise choice based on a proper evaluation of the circumstances. A man or a woman who possesses evaluating faith knows how to arrive at a proper decision.

Eldridge Clever, the famous Black Panther, who was involved in many terrorist activities and who fled our country to live in communist countries for many years, became a Christian and returned home to preach in what he came to call "the best country in the world." May God give you evaluating faith today.

Our Sacrificial Staff

We have some wonderful people who have felt called of God to live on our campground here in Virginia. The life here is not luxurious—to say the very least. Everyone who lives here works very hard and spends long hours preparing for and serving the many people who come from overseas and from our own country to seek God in the regular campmeetings. But these sacrificial people are here because they've made a conscious choice to serve the Lord in this very special way. Furthermore, most of us would not trade the life we have here for anything else in the world. We have evaluated the pros and cons, and this choice is the result.

God Needed a Deliverer

God had heard the cry of His people in bondage in Egypt and needed a man to deliver them, but the choice was up to Moses. No one can force you to fast and pray and study God's Word. No one can force you to live a disciplined and productive life. You have to choose it based on a personal evaluation of everything involved.

It's a very personal choice and can only be made as you *"set your affection on things above"*:

> *Set your affection on things above, not on things on the earth.* Colossians 3:2

Moses' evaluating faith enabled him to make the right decision.

Willing to Be Among "the Lord's Despised Few"

We used to sing the old hymn:

> *I'm going through, I'm going through.*
> *I'll pay the price whatever others do.*
> *I'll take the way of the Lord's despised few.*
> *I'm going through, brother,*
> *I'm going through.*

Then, we noticed that the newer hymnals were changing the words of the chorus. Instead of "the Lord's despised few," their new version said "the Lord's triumphant few." Well, there's nothing wrong with being triumphant, but if we choose to serve the Lord faithfully, we'll also know what it is to be despised in this world at times.

Don't Let Your Suffering Be Your Own Fault

Some people bring reproach upon themselves by their foolishness and lack of wisdom, and there is no reward for bearing this type of reproach. God cannot bless us when we put our brothers and sisters in danger by our own foolish actions.

Boldness must never be confused with stupidity. I know that God sometimes speaks to us to do unusual things, but just be sure it's God and not your own foolish idea.

If you act on your own, God is never obligated to bail you out of your trouble. If you do something for His sake, He'll be with you every step of the way and will give you certain victory. So, let evaluating faith rise in your heart today. It's time to start *LIVING BY FAITH*.

Chapter 6

Separating Faith

By faith he forsook Egypt, not fearing the wrath of the king: for he endured, as seeing him who is invisible. Hebrews 11:27

There comes a time when you have to separate yourself from those who are of a different philosophy of life. As a believer, you now want to be around those who think like you think, act like you act, and talk like you talk.

Some Separation Is Automatic

Sometimes this separation is done for us. For instance, I didn't have to leave my old crowd when I got saved; they just didn't want to have any more to do with me. They knew that what I had was real, but they wanted no part of it. There's always a separation that takes place when we believe, and if it doesn't come automatically, then we must do the separating ourselves for the sake of our souls.

As we noted in an earlier chapter, Egypt was a type of the world and a type of sin, so Moses chose to forsake it. Your faith cannot operate in the world. It cannot operate in the natural realm, only in the realm of the Spirit. The natural world, just as the natural mind, is the enemy of God:

> *Because the carnal mind is enmity against God: for it is not subject to the law of God, neither indeed can be.* Romans 8:7

Therefore, if you are to prosper spiritually, you must stay as far away from the world as possible.

Stay Well Back from the Edge

The story is told of a wealthy man who was looking for a new carriage driver, and three men answered his ad. He said to each of them in turn, "As a test of your driving ability, I want you to see how close you can come to that cliff over there."

The first man came within three feet of the cliff. "I can see that you're an experienced driver," the rich man told him. "I'll let you know when I've made my final decision."

The next man did even better. He came within a foot of the cliff and was given the same answer.

The third man, however, was not so daring. He didn't think any job was worth risking his life near a cliff, so he kept himself at a safe distance. It was this man who was hired on the spot. Keep as far away from danger as you can. Don't flirt with tragedy. Don't risk your spiritual life for momentary pleasures. Learn to have separating faith.

You can't rub elbows with the devil or his crowd without something rubbing off on you. Moses didn't waste any time in getting out of Egypt. He fled—*"by faith."* So put on your track shoes and run as fast as you can run. And run as far as you can run before you stop. Put as much distance between yourself and the world as you possibly can. That's wisdom, and that's faith. Get out of there and stay out of there, and you'll find God's favor upon your life.

Insist on Being Around Someone Who Can Speak Positive Words into Your Life

Insist on being around someone who will tell you that you can. Stay around people who will lead you forward, and stay away from those who are going backward. Don't be joined to those who are doing things halfway.

"God said I could do it and get away with it," many are saying. You stay away from them, for they're headed for disaster. The greatest miracles in the Bible happened in the life of Moses, and it was all because he had separating faith.

It's not unusual for those who make a decision to serve God to be disinherited by their parents and relatives, but it's worth it all. It's a price worth paying—whatever the cost. Don't compromise for any person, and don't compromise for any thing.

Lot Was Called to Separate Himself and His Family

An angel of the Lord warned Lot to get out of Sodom and to go to a mountain. Lot was afraid and wanted, instead, to go to another nearby city. It was just a small town, but he was sure he would be safe there. When the angel told him that his only hope of deliverance was to flee to the mountain, he was saddened, for he didn't want to go there. It was only the next morning, when Lot saw fire and brimstone beginning to fall from Heaven, that he finally became willing to flee to higher ground.

SEPARATING FAITH

Deliverance is in the mountain. We must separate ourselves from the people of sin, the places of sin, and the habits of sin. Flee to the mountain, for joy will be found there.

Egypt Was the "In" Place

In Moses' time, people came to Egypt from every other nation on the earth, for the whole world looked to Egypt for leadership. Egypt was the "in" place of the day. Still, Moses couldn't wait to get out of there. The book of Revelation mentions the death of the two witnesses in a city *"which spiritually is called ... Egypt"*:

> *And their dead bodies shall lie in the street of the great city, which spiritually is called Sodom and Egypt, where also our Lord was crucified.* Revelation 11:8

We know that Jesus was crucified in Jerusalem, but when Jerusalem is taken over by the Antichrist and is used for evil purposes, God will no longer call it the Holy City. Instead, He will call it *"Sodom and Egypt."*

71

Avoid Compromising Churches

A great number of churches have changed their stance on the Rapture and now say that it will never occur. I'm personally convinced that the reason for their change of heart is that they're living so close to the world that the very thought of leaving this world is too painful for them. Their homes and automobiles are so nice that they just can't bear the thought of parting with them. They've worked so hard to build up their social standing in the community that the thought of losing it is painful to them. It happened to Lot and his family too.

Mrs. Lot was the president of the local women's club and had tea at her house every Wednesday afternoon. Lot himself was head of the local chamber of commerce, and as a successful businessman, he was sought out by the young men of the community and became their advisor. As a result, Mrs. Lot simply couldn't bear the thought of leaving behind all that they had in Sodom. She knew that the Lord had sent an angel with a warning and exactly what his messages were, but she couldn't get her mind off of the things that were being left behind and kept wondering if there might not be some way to save them. This led to her turning back and becoming a pillar of salt, a constant reminder for all generations to come that we must not get too attached to the things of this world, which are only loaned to us for a short time.

Separation can be very painful. But if we believe that we're giving up a lesser thing to gain a greater, the pain of it fades as the morning mist.

Lot Was Spared Only by the Mercy of God

The fact is that Lot and his wife and their daughters were only spared by the mercy of God. None of them wanted to leave Sodom. One angel had to take Mr. Lot by one hand and Mrs. Lot by the other hand, while the other angel took the two daughters by the hand. And, in this way, angels actually led them all out of Sodom like little children. Sadly, only Lot and his daughters reached safety. Mrs. Lot never made it.

Moses didn't make the same mistake. He was eager to leave Egypt. The world had lost its glamor and attraction for him, and nothing could hold him back. He had caught a glimpse of something better, and he would not be denied. He had refusing faith, choosing faith, evaluating faith and separating faith.

Two Methods of Separation

There are two methods of separation: God can force you to separate, or you can do it willingly. If you're forced to obey, I'm convinced, you lose half of the blessing.

If Abraham had not been willing to be separated from Ur and from his family and friends, he could not have become the father of faith. If Ruth had refused to leave Moab and her people, she would never have joined the lineage of Jesus and been praised by all succeeding generations. She chose not to do the comfortable thing, but to do what God had put in her heart to do.

Leaving familiar surroundings, leaving a stable job and income, leaving loved ones ... none of these are pleasant experiences. But without separation (when and if God requires it) there can be no permanent victory.

Ruth did not dwell on the separation from her people. Instead, she said to her mother-in-law:

SEPARATING FAITH

"Thy people shall be my people." She was not tormented over being the first to break the religious tradition of her people. Instead, she said, *"Thy God shall be my God."* She was not unduly concerned about where and how she would live in a strange land. Instead, she said, *"Whither thou lodgest, I will lodge."* In fact, she was so decided that separation was God's will for her that she pleaded with her mother-in-law not to insist that she stay behind:

> *Entreat me not to leave thee, or to return from following after thee.*   Ruth 1:16

Ruth had separating faith, and it made her a great woman. It takes faith to forsake the familiar and the comfortable to launch out into the unknown, but it brings great rewards every time.

It doesn't just happen automatically. You have to make it happen. And it's time to start *Living by Faith.*   ⟿

Chapter 7

Fearless Faith

By faith he forsook Egypt, not fearing the wrath of the king: for he endured, as seeing him who is invisible. Hebrews 11:27

Moses had a fearless faith. He was not afraid of what the pharaoh would do or say. And that is truly amazing. This pharaoh was an extremely powerful man with great resources at his disposal. He was the type of man you surely wouldn't want to make your enemy.

Faith Conquers Every Fear

Only faith could explain Moses' lack of fear in this situation. Only God can give a person that kind of assurance, so that they can say, like Paul:

> *What shall we then say to these things? If*
> *God be for us, who can be against us?*
>
> Romans 8:31

We must not be restrained because of fear of the local school board. We must not be hesitant because of fear of religious leaders. God has called us to be bold in the face of every opposition. He said:

> *And fear not them which kill the body, but*
> *are not able to kill the soul: but rather fear*
> *him which is able to destroy both soul and*
> *body in hell.* Matthew 10:28

> *But I will forewarn you whom ye shall fear:*
> *Fear him, which after he hath killed hath*
> *power to cast into hell; yea, I say unto you,*
> *Fear him.* Luke 12:5

The Secret of Moses' Fearlessness

What made Moses so fearless? Thank God the secret of his fearlessness is stated clearly in the Scriptures. He could do it because he was *"seeing Him who is invisible."* His knowledge of the greatness of God overshadowed every other consideration. His knowledge of the power of God overcame every obstacle.

Knowing and seeing God was all he had, but if you can catch a glimpse of Him, every fear will fade into nothingness. Seeing God became Moses' motivation in life, and if you can catch a glimpse of Him, it will turn your life around too.

So Moses had refusing faith, choosing faith, evaluating faith, separating faith, and fearless faith. This enabled him to live by faith every day, resulting in some of the greatest miracles the Bible records. How about you? It's time to start *LIVING BY FAITH*.

Wallace H. Heflin, Jr.
1932-1996

He loved to preach in the Old Gospel Tent ....

Washington, D.C, North Carolina and Virgina were
frequently blessed by the presence of the tent.

More than anything, he loved to pray for people, believing that if he got his hands on them, they would never be the same again. And they weren't!

He loved China ...

On the Great Wall of China!

Praying for the Chinese church.

... and went there dozens of times.

At the tomb of Sun Yat Sen.

With his mother on the wall.

Russia and Israel, ...

Preaching in Red Square in Moscow.

... two more of his frequent destinations

Overlooking the
city of Jesusalem, a
city he loved and
visited often, usually
twice every year.

An all of the rest of the nations of the world were his parish.

Praying for crippled children in Africa.

With his Sister, Ruth Ward Heflin, and their mutual long-time friend, Gwen Shaw, founder of End-Time Handmaidens.

Part III

Lessons in Faith from an Unnamed Woman

Chapter 8

How Faith Works

And a certain woman, which had an issue of blood twelve years, and had suffered many things of many physicians, and had spent all that she had, and was nothing bettered, but rather grew worse, when she had heard of Jesus, came in the press behind, and touched his garment. For she said, If I may touch but his clothes, I shall be whole. And straightway the fountain of her blood was dried up; and she felt in her body that she was healed of that plague.

And Jesus, immediately knowing in himself that virtue had gone out of him, turned him about in the press, and said, Who touched my clothes?

And his disciples said unto him, Thou seest the multitude thronging thee, and sayest thou, Who touched me?

And he looked round about to see her that had done this thing. But the woman fearing and trembling, knowing what was done in her, came and fell down before him, and told him all the truth. And he said unto her, Daughter, thy faith hath made thee whole; go in peace, and be whole of thy plague.

Mark 5:25-34

The case of the woman with the issue of blood is a classic example of faith in so many respects. She put her faith into action by certain things that she said and did, and we must do the same. And we don't even know her name.

Twelve Years of Suffering Is Too Much

This woman, for twelve years, had an issue of blood. In other words, she was hemorrhaging, and it had gone on for a very long time. She went from one doctor to the other, and the Scriptures say that instead of getting better, she actually got worse. Not only did her physical condition deteriorate, but her financial condition deteriorated as well. Now, she was not only sick, but she was also poor.

She had spent all her money trying to be healed, and instead of getting better, she had only gotten worse. Thank God she heard about Jesus.

Tell It Everywhere

It's important for every one of us to tell what Jesus is doing in our lives. Others need to hear it, so that they can come to Jesus and know that He is able to deliver them and set them free. When we fail to tell what our glorious Lord is doing, we rob others who are in need of Him. There are hundreds and even thousands of sick people who might be healed if we would only let them know that Jesus is still in the healing business.

I'm so glad that He's not building hospitals, that He hasn't turned His work over to clinics and the men and women who run them. He's still in the healing business and still doing the thing He died on the cross to do.

I'm so glad He hasn't turned my salvation over to someone else, so glad I don't have to go to someone else to get saved. I don't believe anyone else could have gotten the job done. And, just as Jesus is not turning salvation over to others, He's also not turning healing over to others. He died for our salvation, and He also died for our healing. When we dare to believe that He's able to do the work, He's ready and waiting to perform the miracle that each of us needs.

A Spark of Faith Overcomes Weakness

Somebody told this woman about Jesus, and she was glad. She was sick and weak. The longer you have a condition like hers, the weaker you get. Still, despite her weakness, this woman began to say within herself (even before she ever left home) those wonderful words of faith: *"If I can but touch the hem of his garment, I shall be made whole."* What powerful words they are!

But faith is put to work by what we say and what we do, and every time you say, "I seem to be getting a terrible headache," then you've got one. Every time you say, "I think I'm getting a backache," then you'll get one. Every time you say, "I think I feel a cold coming on," or "It seems like I'm getting a good case of hay fever," then you'll get a cold or a good case of hay fever. Why? Because you're confessing it, and thus claiming it as being yours. We must begin to resist the devil and rebuke him and not receive those things that he's trying to bring upon us. When you do this, you'll see faith begin to operate, warding off all that the enemy tries to bring.

Go Where God Is Working

That woman said in her spirit, "If I can just get there. If I can just touch the hem of His garment, I know that I will be made every whit whole."

If you're sick and weary in body and there's a service that night at your church, don't you dare stay home. Instead, do the same thing this woman did and say the same thing she said. "I know I'm not feeling well, but I'm sure that as soon as I get to church and begin to lift my hands and my voice in praise and worship unto God, He'll do the work, and I'll be made whole."

Then get in your car and go to church, and before you get inside the door, you'll begin to feel the delivering power of Almighty God. Why? Because you've believed that it would be so. When any man or woman goes to church to be delivered, they will not leave disappointed.

When you begin to tell others about what God is doing, you'll find some hungry hearts. And what you're telling them will be as water to their thirsty souls.

When I was preaching in Rocky Mount, North Carolina, one year, one of the ladies who was attending the meetings testified to her neighbor, a lady terribly afflicted with arthritis, and as a result that lady came to the meeting also. If there ever was a night I wished I'd had a television camera rolling, it was that night.

By the time I got ready to preach, the Lord had already spoken. He had said, "I have come to give you miracles." As I started to read my scripture, the Lord spoke to me and said, "I told you that I've come to give you miracles." I stopped reading, and immediately started to minister to the people. When I came to that woman, I found that her hands were terribly stiff. In fact, every joint of her body was stiff with arthritis. She told me a very pitiful story.

She had been craving some cabbage, and she tried to fix some, but she was unable to hold the knife. She decided to just put the cabbage into the pan as it was, without cutting it up, but when she had the cabbage in the pan, she couldn't hold on to the pan, and it dropped to the floor before she could get it to the stove. She would have no cabbage that day.

She'd had to quit her work because she could no longer perform the simplest tasks, but while she was standing there in her misery, Jesus came and delivered her from the top of her head to the soles of her feet. And when it happened, I promise you that you've never seen such carrying on in your life. Candid Camera would have loved to film her.

We were all so thrilled for this woman and blessed just to see how she appreciated the hand of God coming and delivering her and setting her free. It was glorious, but it never would have happened if someone had not told her what Jesus was doing in the revival meetings.

Friend, in all the neighborhoods around about you, there are people who are bound and need to be delivered by the power of God. If you and I will dare to tell them that Jesus is moving and doing the work, it will be done.

Go Where Jesus Is

This woman heard that something was happening, and she went to the place where it was happening. You have to go where Jesus is.

Someone might say, "Well, doesn't Jesus work in every place?" Not really. The Bible speaks of

LIVING BY FAITH

places that have Ichabod written over the door, for the Spirit of God has departed from them.

There are many churches today that are churches in name only. There isn't much of God's Spirit in them because they're teaching little more than a socialized gospel. Their preaching is about something that appears on the front page of the newspaper. They don't believe in being born again of the Spirit of God, or in the power of Christ's blood to save. So how can the Spirit of the Lord be there when the Word of God is not preached? You have to go where something's happening, someplace where the waters are troubled.

This woman heard, and then she acted on what she had heard. She went to where Jesus was.

Be Desperate and Determined

When she got there, she encountered a serious problem. The crowd gathered around Jesus was so great that she couldn't see any way of passing through it. At that point, she could easily have said, "Oh, I'm too weak to even make the effort," and she could have gone home the same way as she came. But she didn't do that.

Instead, this woman, filled with faith, began pressing through the crowd. She used every ounce of strength she had because she was desperate and determined, and that's not a bad combination. When we get desperate and begin to scrape the bottom of the barrel, our prayers become more passionate, and God hears us. Sometimes we don't get desperate enough until all hope seems to be gone.

I don't understand why it is that we turn to Jesus only after a physician has said, "I'm sorry, but I've done everything I can for you; there's just nothing more to try." Then, in that moment, we get busy and start crying out to Jesus, and the truth is that He's been waiting for our desperate call all the time.

Nevertheless, Jesus is always there, and He's waiting to minister to us, not just physically, but in every other area of our lives as well. If you need a financial miracle, He's there. If you need wisdom on your job, He's there. If you need restoration for your family, He's there. Whatever you need, He's there to hear and answer your cry. We just need to get to the place where Jesus is manifesting His power, and then we'll see God, as He begins to work for us.

Know How to Approach God

How can you get to God? You don't always have to attend a major crusade or some revival service. You can get to Him right in your own home. He's in your kitchen, your bedroom, and your den.

And how can you make intimate contact with Him? Just lift your hands and your voice to Him, and begin to thank Him for all that He's done. As you begin to praise Him, something wonderful takes place. Why? Because, the Scriptures teach, He inhabits the praises of His people:

> *But thou art holy, O thou that inhabitest the*
> *praises of Israel.*   Psalm 22:3

Through praise, the Lord will come down right where you are and minister to you, and you can be healed and delivered right there. This is the secret for entering into God's presence.

Most of us are guilty of coming to God like beggars. Before we even greet Him or tell Him how much we love Him, before we thank Him for what He's already done for us, we start begging Him for our present need. "Oh, God, I need my car payment, and I need my insurance payment too. And

100

HOW FAITH WORKS

You know I need some money for groceries. The kids just went back to school, and they need to have shoes. The girls need dresses, and the boys need a new pair of pants."

We ask and ask and ask, and we beg and beg and beg, and all of this before we declare our love and appreciation for our Lord. That's not right. In fact, it's just the opposite of right. We may spend a few moments thanking God, but we spend much more time begging from Him. Try reversing that. Spend the majority of your time speaking words of love and appreciation to God, and you'll receive twice as much and get it more quickly.

As we learn to praise our Lord as He is worthy to be praised, then we can feel when the time is right to reach in and take from His bounty. And we never have to be afraid to ask largely. In fact, we can ask for all that we need. It takes exactly the same miracle to give us half a loaf of bread as it does to give us a full loaf. My sister Ruth insists that we usually ask for toys when we should be asking for nations.

God's looking for people who will believe Him for their city, their state, and their country. Do you believe that your city, your state, or your nation has gone too far from God and cannot ever experience revival again? Draw close to God, and then dare to be bold with your petitions for those around you. When you do, He will do the work.

Push Past Every Obstacle

This woman pressed her way through the crowd. She didn't just stand calmly by and say to the people around her, "Excuse me, please. Could I get through?" She bent down on her hands and knees and began to push and wiggle her way through the crowd, under and between them all until ... wonder of wonders, she was able to make her way to Jesus. Then, the Scriptures tell us, she reached out and touched the hem of His garment, and when she did this, virtue went out of Him and into her.

I've prayed for people, and when I got through ministering to them, I was left so weak that I had to sit down. It seemed that every bit of strength had gone out of me, and so I understand how Jesus felt when virtue went out of Him." Life flowed out of Him and into that woman who for twelve long years had suffered a condition for which men said there was no hope. When she touched Jesus, she not only received hope; she received the impossible.

Reach Out and Touch the Lord

Immediately, Jesus turned and began looking for the person who had touched Him. The disciples couldn't understand this. They said, "Master, the crowd is pressing in all around You, and You say that someone has touched You?"

In any crowd, there are often only a few who press through and actually touch the Lord. I'm sure all of us have had the experience of seeing God move mightily and then looking around us and seeing other people totally bored with it all or actually falling asleep. Great things were happening, but they didn't press into them. They're just there, spectators occupying seats, but they don't know how to enter into the presence of God, and they don't understand why everybody else is shouting and rejoicing and getting happy in Jesus. Jesus said, "Someone has touched Me." Let that someone be you today.

Today, each and every one of us can touch Him, and if we do, we'll receive exactly what we're seeking Him for. Each of us has different needs, and God has what we need. Stop asking for trinkets and start asking for serious blessings. Ask largely, and dare to believe God for the answer.

Is the Lord Ever Too Busy to Bless You?

When this miracle took place, Jesus was on His way to the house of Jairus, the ruler of the synagogue. That fact could have discouraged this woman. She could have thought she had no right to meet the Lord and receive from Him, for she was just a poor woman, with no apparent reputation to precede her. "This man is on His way to the house of an important dignitary. He doesn't have time for me. I'd better leave Him alone." Still, her need was so great that, like blind Bartimaeus on the road to Jericho, she was compelled to cry out to Him.

"Oh, thou son of David," Bartimaeus cried, *"Have mercy on me."* And in that moment, Jesus stood still just for that one man. Now, Jesus was there to minister to this woman in her hour of need. He delivered her and set her free, and she went on her way rejoicing, telling of all the great things He had done. If you'll just dare to let your faith be released, you'll see God, as He begins to work for you too.

F-A-I-T-H

We spell faith, F-A-I-T-H. It stands for: Forsaking all, I take Him. Many people receive little from

God because they are double-minded, and the Bible tells us:

> *But let him ask in faith, nothing wavering. For he that wavereth is like a wave of the sea driven with the wind and tossed. For let not that man think that he shall receive any thing of the Lord. A double-minded man is unstable in all his ways.* James 1:6-8

I've had people come to me and say, "I'm scheduled to be operated on on Tuesday, and if God doesn't heal me tonight, I'm going to the hospital tomorrow." Then they wonder why they don't get delivered. They're saying, "Jesus, I'm coming, but if You don't do it, I've got a doctor who will operate." Trust God completely, and you'll be healed. F-A-I-T-H also means: Forsaking all, I trust Him.

Let God Get All the Glory

A number of years ago, I was taking a group to the Holy Land, and among them was an elderly sister of about eighty. She had a back condition and used a cane for support as she walked. She had bought two boxes of St. Joseph's aspirin because she had more faith in St. Joseph's than she did in Jesus. When we were in the airport in Rome, she held two aspirin she was about to take in one hand and the two boxes of aspirin in the other hand, and then asked me to pray for her.

Pointing to the aspirins, I said, "What are you going to do with those?"

She said, "I'm going to take them."

But I knew that if I would pray for her, Jesus would heal her, and who would get all the credit but good old St. Joseph's? So I said, "Give me those aspirin."

She said, "Oh, no, I can't do that."

I said, "Sister, we're going to be together seventeen days, and you're going to need my prayers many times in those seventeen days. If you agree to give me the aspirin, then I'll pray."

She said, "Oh, no! I need the aspirin." I believe she would have given me all her money before she would have parted with those aspirins, and I didn't want aspirins to get the credit for what God was going to do. I wanted her to trust in Jesus. After much coaxing, she agreed to rely only on Jesus, and I finally got the aspirins—although you would have thought I was taking her arm off.

She handed me both boxes of aspirin, and I began to pray. While I was still speaking my prayer, she shot out from under my hand and started running through the airport, and I don't think I could have caught her. She was healed. Let's stop being double-minded about the things of God. Dare to trust Him and say with Job:

> *Though he slay me, yet will I trust in him.*
> Job 13:15

God has never done any of us damage yet. He's always there to bring us deliverance when we need it. But it is as we learn the secret of faith that God will begin to move in and through our lives. It doesn't matter what the need.

If you have faith in God, He will perform the thing He has spoken unto your life. And let that faith affect everything you do. It's time to start *LIVING BY FAITH.*

Part IV

The Faith *You* Need

Chapter 9

Increasing Faith

*But grow in grace, and in the knowledge of
our Lord and Saviour Jesus Christ. To him
be glory both now and for ever. Amen.*

2 Peter 3:18

You need faith and you need more faith, so you
need to keep your faith fresh and growing.

Your Faith Should
Be Constantly Rising

As you *"grow in grace"* and as you grow *"in the
knowledge of our Lord and Saviour Jesus Christ,"*
your faith should be constantly rising as well. As
you learn more about Jesus, you will come to
know His goodness, His total faithfulness, and the
power of the Word He has spoken. This should
begin as early in life as possible.

111

Teaching Your Children Faith

It's wonderful when we can get a start on faith in childhood. If you want your children to be people of faith, begin to instill faith in them now. Begin to teach them while they're still young.

Moses was blessed to be taught faith by his believing parents:

> *By faith Moses, when he was born, was hid three months of his parents, because they saw he was a proper child; and they were not afraid of the king's commandment.*
>
> Hebrews 11:23

What a blessing! Those of us who were born of Christian parents are fortunate because something very special was ingrained in us from an early age. As I noted early on, I am particularly blessed because I was born of two old-time Pentecostal pastors, parents who lived faith and taught faith. My life might have been very different otherwise.

This faith can be instilled in subtle ways. For instance, when a child falls down and hurts himself or herself, he or she runs to Mama for comfort. Mama, if you will have a word of prayer in that moment and speak a word of faith to your child, you'll do much to lay a proper foundation for the future faith of that little one. The most important thing to that child is how you react to their falling down. If you believe that they're going to be healed, your calm and assurance will be communicated to them. If you get all upset and worried in that critical moment, they'll get another message entirely.

My older sister, Betty, died when her four children were still small. When those children would fall down and skin a knee or an arm or burn themselves, they would sometimes come running to me—if I happened to be closer than Grandma. I would lay hands on them and pray for them. Then I would always give them a little slap on that spot, and they would go on their way happy that things were going to be okay. And they always were. The pain disappeared, the soreness went out of the wound, and the child was fine.

A child is capable of learning and of exercising great faith. It is a simple faith and simple faith is powerful. If we allow such a faith to develop in our children, it's the greatest thing we can do for them. This was the blessing Moses enjoyed.

Have Childlike Faith

Children have great faith for finances. The daughter of one of our pastors came forward in a special meeting and pledged $100.00. Then, from that day, she began to look every day for the mailman to come, to see how God was going to supply her $100.00 she had promised to give. One day someone handed me an envelope with $100.00 in it and said, "This is for the pastor's girl. I want to pay her pledge." We might think that some grown-up was just feeling sorry for a child who had made a foolish mistake, but I don't believe it for a moment. God used that person to supply a child's need. It happened because of her simple, childlike faith.

Childlike faith produces miracles, and that particular child will never forget what God did for her that day.

A thirteen-year-old boy took a camp pledge envelope. A couple of weeks later his older sister came weeping to the altar saying, "I want to pay my brother's pledge." How many know that sisters don't normally do that? That boy's faith produced a miracle, for when a child shows faith, God must honor that faith.

INCREASING FAITH

The faith that caused Moses, in later years, to lead the nation of Israel, a faith that produced some of the greatest miracles recorded in sacred scripture, was instilled in him as a boy at his mother's knee. Never underestimate the faith of a child.

When your children hear you speaking faith and see you acting in faith, it will become a part of them. And when they're older, the faith they've learned from you will help them to face life's challenges successfully.

Both Fear and Faith Are Contagious

Moses had a great heritage. His parents were *"not afraid of the king's commandment."* Fear is communicated; it is contagious. If you react in fear and are threatened by life's circumstances, your children will sense your fear and be afraid too.

Faith is also contagious. When you stand firm, no matter what happens, and say, "We will stand on the Lord's side, and nothing will harm us," you'll impart that same faith to your loved ones.

But you must begin early. What will happen to your children if you fail to impart faith to them? The Bible says:

> *Train up a child in the way he should go:*
> *and when he is old, he will not depart from*
> *it.*   Proverbs 22:6

And the opposite is also true.

I'm an example of the truth of Proverbs 22:6, a product of that godly philosophy. When I tried to run from God, I never got very far. My parents' prayers always brought me back. The faith they had instilled in me early bore fruit.

Even Adults Need Increasing Faith

Even as adults, we want to see our faith increasing on a regular basis. That growth can sometimes be more easily understood if we put it in practical terms. If you have twenty-dollar faith and you need $15.00, that's no problem for you. God has given you $15.00 before, and you know that He'll do it again.

If you need $50.00, however, that presents a problem. Your faith must rise to a new level. Some people get all perturbed at that point and wonder where the $50.00 will come from. But when God presents us with such a challenge, we should accept it as an opportunity to enlarge and strengthen our faith, and we should be grateful for it. If we fast and pray and seek His face that our faith might be stretched, at the eleventh hour and the fifty-ninth minute, He will give us the $50.00 we need.

When that happens, you will now have fifty-dollar faith, and when you need $25.00, that's nothing for you. Even when you need $50.00, it's no problem. You know that God has done it once, and you're confident that He'll do it again.

But when a $100.00 need arises, again your faith is challenged. Don't be discouraged when this happens. God has not allowed it for your destruction. He is giving you a new opportunity for growth. So don't despair, and don't worry. Have faith in God. Some people nearly have a breakdown "praying in" what they need. Relax and let God do a miracle for you.

When God meets this need, you will then have hundred-dollar faith and can go on to greater things. No wonder the enemy fights your advance! He fears great faith and will do anything and everything to stop it.

I can remember the time when I stayed awake at night wondering how the Lord would supply our needs at camp. At that time, we needed about

$50.00 a day. Now $50.00 a day won't buy even the bread we use. Sometimes the bread alone costs $165.00 or more.

Once you have hundred-dollar faith, if you need $50.00, that's not a problem. If you need $75.00, that doesn't bother you. But when you need $200.00, then the stretching begins again. Don't despise God's attempts to lift you to a higher level of faith. Keep growing. Keep developing.

Let Your Faith Be Increased

Once, God spoke to an Australian pastor and said, "You're believing Me for only the tithe of what I want to give you." He was surprised, because he had thousand-dollar faith. When I arrived at his place to preach, the Lord told me to raise $10,000.00 for him. He had a campground and men available to build on it, but he had no materials for doing the building. God wanted to give him $10,000.00, and his faith had been for $1,000.00.

I believe that most of us are in this same condition. We have limited God by our limited vision. Let your faith be a growing faith, an ever-expanding faith.

As a minister of the Gospel, you can't spend

your time believing for your groceries, for your light bill, and for your heating oil. There's nothing wrong with believing for those things, but you have to set your sights higher. You must begin to believe God for nations and peoples.

I can't spend my time praying for money for gasoline when nations are ripe for revival. I have to raise my sights higher. I don't spend my time praying for food to eat. I do very well in that category. If you spend all your time praying for the necessities of life, you will never have enough faith to reach out to hurting and suffering people around the world. Lift your sights, and let God increase your faith.

We must believe God for television programs and missionary outreaches, so please don't spend all your time praying for the mundane things of life. And how can you get away from that isolation? Begin praying for others, trusting God that as you concern yourself for them, He will take care of you.

Pray for your church and your pastor. Pray for the ministers of America. Pray for the churches of the world. If you'll get this increased vision, you'll never again have to worry about the light bill, the grocery bill, and the car payment. Your faith will have risen to a new height in God and will be producing much more than you need for yourself.

Laugh at Your Yesterdays

As your faith grows, you can laugh at the smaller problems of life. They become rather comical. Just as you look back and laugh at your first attempts to take a few steps as a child or to begin speaking, you can later laugh at yourself and the struggles you had in your life of faith just a short time ago.

These things are humorous now because you've grown so far beyond them. And when others come to you with the same problems, you can encourage them and help them through their trials because you know that these are only passing trials that we can all face and overcome.

We can actually laugh at the devil—when we come to know that God's power is so much greater than his, when we realize how limited the enemy is, and when we realize our true potential in Christ. Looking back on the trials of yesterday, we realize that we really had nothing at all to worry about. Our God was always bigger than our current problems, and we were always destined to have victory in Him.

When your faith has grown, you're not only able to encourage others in their faith, but you're actually able to reach down and pick them up and strengthen them. You have seen God work in a similar situation, and you know that He'll do it again. If He got Daniel out of the lions' den, He can do it again.

You're Limited by the Level of Your Faith

You can never think the thoughts of God or act in accordance with the mind of God in any greater measure than the level of faith that you possess at the moment. If you still have that twenty-five-dollar faith, you'll not be able to comprehend the greatness of what God is about to do in those hundred-dollar and five-hundred-dollar situations. Those thoughts are still too great for you.

The Scriptures tell us to *"bring into captivity every thought to the obedience of Christ"* (2 Corinthians 10:5). When you allow your faith to rise, your fleshly thought processes are moved aside, and you begin to take off the limitations and understand more of the mind of Christ. Eventually, you'll know that nothing is impossible with God.

When you've risen only slightly in faith and you overhear someone talking of going on radio or television with their ministry, you can't comprehend how it could be possible.

In a church in the southern part of America, the pastor somehow could not catch the vision of how to go about preaching on the radio. In his mind, the church just couldn't afford it. Then two of his members (two good sisters) believed God and started a radio program of their own. Their faith challenged him, and then he, too, began a radio ministry.

"I don't think I can do that," someone may say.

"I believe it wouldn't be wise to try it," another may agree.

"Don't even think about it," the devil will argue. "It would be sheer pride for you to attempt such a thing. Who are you anyway?"

But then someone else comes along and, simply laughing at the devil, goes about doing it, and God works for them.

Faith Brings Understanding

Your understanding of what God can do and what He wants to do will come in the same measure as the increase of your faith in Him. As you learn to appropriate what you now have revealed, He will show you new things to appropriate. Be bold to take on new levels of faith, and grow into new dimensions in God.

There was a time when believing God for a new car was just more than I could muster. I drove old cars for more than twenty years. As the cost of automobiles rose rapidly, I thought less and less about buying a new one. But then God caused my faith to rise so sharply by sending me to the nations that believing Him for a new automobile became a simple thing. So, in recent years, He has given me several beautiful automobiles that I could use for His glory. Nothing is too hard for our God.

There are always a dozen needs, but force your faith. Reach beyond the impossibilities to the things that are needed in your ministry. When you need an organ, believe God to supply it. When you need a piano, believe Him to act on your behalf. When He shows you that you need to be on television, He's more than able to make a way for you to do it. God never tells you to do something you are incapable of doing.

Step Onto Another Level of Faith

When you learn faith from someone else, the advantage is that you don't have to start at the bottom and work your way up. You can absorb the faith the person teaching you has already accumulated, and you can start rising from the position of their faith. If you're willing to sit at the feet of men and women of faith, it's possible to jump onto the level of faith they have attained and be ready to move on up from there to even greater things in God.

When you're new on any job, you're assigned the most menial tasks so that you can learn the work from the ground up. But in the arena of faith, we can take great leaps in understanding and position, through absorbing the faith lessons others present to us.

I didn't have to repeat the sacrifices my parents went through more than fifty years ago, and you don't have to repeat the sacrifices I went through in my early years of ministry. Move onto the level of faith being preached and lived today.

When you approach an apartment building on a hill, and a walk leads up to what seems to be the main entrance, you may think that you're entering on the ground level. But what you can't see from your vantage point is that there are three other stories under the one you're entering, and because of the lay of the land, you're actually entering on the third floor.

Faith is like that. You can enter at the level some great teacher or preacher of faith is living, although they have pioneered and laid the foundations and have other levels under that. If you can learn to jump onto the level others are presently on, you'll be able to take great leaps in your life of faith in God.

Faith can be appropriated in this way by the one who is listening, because he or she can say, "If it works for them, it will work for me." And, since God has assured us that He is *"no respecter of persons"* (Acts 10:34), they're right. Faith makes you know that if God will give me miracles, He'll give you miracles too. If He'll answer my prayers, He'll answer your prayers too. What God has done for one He will do for another—if we can just believe Him for it. Moving forward in God demands an ever-increasing trust in the Almighty, so it's time to start *Living by Faith.* ✎

Chapter 10

Tested Faith

... that the trial of your faith, being much more precious than of gold that perisheth, though it be tried with fire, might be found unto praise and honour and glory at the appearing of Jesus Christ.   1 Peter 1:7

One of the most important ways your faith grows and stays fresh is through the troubling situations presented by life. Growing faith requires regular testing, and the testing of your faith promotes growth.

Faith Will Always Be Tested

There are two reasons your faith will always be tested. The first is that when God is moving, the devil is always there trying to prevent His will from being accomplished. When you step out to do something for God, you can know that opposition will surely come. Satan doesn't care how he does it, just so he stops you. He will use anything, and nothing is beneath him.

He will use your children. They might get sick. At Christmastime, the enemy may tell you that you can't have a good Christmas if you serve God. "You'll never have any money," he'll say. Know that he'll speak any lie that serves his purpose.

But never despise the tests through which you pass—whatever form they happen to take. Even when Satan is active in your test, God is behind it and will not permit Satan to test you beyond your spiritual capability. This is His promise:

> *There hath no temptation taken you but such as is common to man: but God is faithful, who will not suffer you to be tempted above that ye are able; but will with the temptation also make a way to escape, that ye may be able to bear it.*
>
> 1 Corinthians 10:13

God knows that your faith can only grow through testing, so He'll permit such tests to come. But they're always for your good, never for your detriment. Trials are a blessing to the person of faith, never a hindrance. When you make up your mind that nothing will hinder your faith, great victories will come to you.

When the devil knows, however, that he can hinder you by bringing the same test and trial as before, he will not hesitate to do it again and again. His job is to keep your spirit in constant turmoil, and he's good at it. But when you have decided that you will trust God come what may, then nothing the enemy can do will turn you aside, and you will be victorious.

If you have children and you've decided to live by faith and trust God, when your children get sick, don't automatically bundle them into the car and head for the doctor's office. Pray for them, expecting God to do a miracle. If you jump every time the devil threatens your children's health, he'll see to it that they stay sick. If you've decided to serve God, lay your hands on your sick children, and God will heal them. This simple act of faith will make all the difference in your life.

A friend who's in Christian television said to me many years ago, "My wife is a nurse. So, when we got saved, the only thing we knew to do when our children got sick was to take them to the doctor or the hospital. It was astounding how much money we spent on their health needs by the end of a year. When we looked back, we saw that every time they'd had a runny nose, we had sought professional help. We decided that we were going to believe God for the healing of our children, and it was amazing how God kept those children well, saving us thousands of dollars in medical bills and giving us peace of mind in the process."

I was blessed because my mother, in raising the three of us, never resorted to medicines or doctors. At a very early age, we were taught that Jesus was our Healer. I fell out of trees, cut myself more than enough times, and contracted the common childhood diseases; but each time we had a physical need, we trusted God. Experiencing sickness is a wonderful arena in which to let your faith be exercised and grow, and if you'll be faithful, God will also do His part.

Failure Requires That You Repeat the Class

Every test you pass will enable you to take an even greater step in God. But if you fail a test, then you'll have to repeat it, sometimes many times.

It's just like attending school. If you fail the third grade, you have to repeat it—or you should anyway—until you get it right.

None of us likes the tests of life, but when we realize that they'll never return if we pass them the first time, it causes us to put forth an extra effort and try to pass them once and for all. Then we can concentrate on moving on to greater things.

Faith Grows by Stretching

Faith grows by stretching and by testing, and that creates problems for some of us. But when you have no trials, how can your faith grow? If you're never tested, how can your faith increase? God has the right to test and try you. He has the right to stretch you, and He does it for your own good.

This stretching will only come when you're in the position that demands it, and if you're never in that position, your faith will never grow. It's ironic. We all want great faith, but we don't want the accompanying great problems. Yet, when you have great faith, you'll never again have a small problem. Your problems will grow in proportion to your increasing faith, for faith must be tested. But don't panic, don't be afraid, and don't worry. Testing is a normal part of the Christian life.

Once your faith begins to rise, small problems will seem as nothing. You'll no longer consider them to be problems at all. And, to God, they're not. They're also not problems to you—if you can only believe. All our problems are God's opportunities. He doesn't get worried about them, and you shouldn't get worried either. He doesn't fret about them, and you shouldn't either.

When your faith takes on new dimensions, it would be foolish for you to continue going through kindergarten tests. Your tests must become more serious now, and that's not a bad thing. You might expect your problems to stop with your increasing faith, but they just get bigger and bigger. However, if you're growing in God, you'll be able to keep on top of the situation and know that God will help you—no matter what comes.

Thirty Years of Ministry Has Brought Significant Changes

I've been saved now and in the ministry for more than thirty years, and I receive much more money now than I did at the first. In fact, there's no comparison. But my responsibilities are also much greater, so my need is greater, and as fast as the money comes in one hand, it goes out the other. Still, God is supplying my every need. There are more places to put it and more things to do with it, so there has to be more of it.

Wouldn't it be sad to have a lesser vision after so many years? That doesn't necessarily mean that we'll have a lot left over. God still supplies according to our need; it's just that our needs are so much greater because of the increased activity for Him. Consequently, we still need to fast and pray and seek God's face, but He is more than able to do exactly what He has promised.

May we never lose this secret of knowing that if we dare to put our trust in Him, He'll always be there to bring us through in victory, and we'll rejoice in the constant manifestation of His goodness.

All Great Men and Women of Faith Came through Great Trials

If you read books about the great men and women of faith of the past, you'll notice that many of them, before moving into the life of great victory, had to come through some great tragedy. Their house burned down, their spouse died, they lost children, they failed in life, on the job, or even in the ministry. William Branham, for instance, lost his wife and family in a tragic accident. T. L. and Daisy Osborn returned from serving as missionaries to India as failures. Maria Woodworth-Etter lost her children, one by one, and then she lost her husband. Still, each of them turned their personal tragedy into great victory by faith, and you can too. The trials of life were not meant to destroy you, but to strengthen your faith and to show you God's goodness. It's time to start *LIVING BY FAITH*.

Chapter 11

Living and Active Faith

Even so faith, if it hath not works, is dead,
being alone.
Wilt thou know, O vain man, that faith
without works is dead?
For as the body without the spirit is dead, so
faith without works is dead also.

James 2:17, 20, and 26

The book of James is one of my favorite books of the Bible because it's so practical and so powerful. James makes it clear that there's a living faith, and there's a dead faith.

Living Faith vs. Dead Faith

There's a faith that is nothing more than talk. It is no longer living, and it produces nothing. It may have once been living, but it is now dead.

Living faith is characterized by the results it produces. It is faith in action. It goes into action and produces something. It is faith accompanied by works. As we noted early in the book, because we seem to be hearing much more preached about faith today than ever before and yet we're seeing little of what real faith ought to produce, we could conclude that there's a lot of dead faith around.

"I don't understand why I didn't get healed," someone says. "I had great faith." But that can't be true, because Jesus said:

> *Verily I say unto you, If ye have faith as a grain of mustard seed, ye shall say unto this mountain, Remove hence to yonder place; and it shall remove; and nothing shall be impossible unto you.*
>
> Matthew 17:20

Great faith always brings forth great results.

There's a difference between faith and mere excitement, a difference between faith and mere emotion. Excitement may dim and emotion may fluctuate, but living and active faith never fails.

God Requires Active Faith

We're all guilty, to some degree, of talking about faith while bringing forth little of the evidence of our faith—the works which living faith must produce. So there is in every one of us some dead faith that must be removed. Living faith cannot be unfruitful, it cannot fail, and it cannot lose. It will always produce results.

"What are you doing now?" I ask some people.

"Oh, we're just waiting for the Lord to move," they answer.

But that's a wrong concept. If you just sit and wait for God to do everything, you may sit around for a very long time, and you may see no results at all. You must move the hand of God by your faith, a living faith, your faith put into action.

When you act in faith, then God must respond. He cannot fail. He never fails to respond to living faith, and He never will fail to respond to it. Living faith always brings victory.

Faith, then, requires something of you. You must act. If you really believe that God is good and that His promises are for you, then you cannot sit still. You must spring into action. And when you spring into action, God is always there to meet you.

The Gifts of the Spirit Never Function Apart from Living and Active Faith

In the matter of the gifts of the Spirit, you must act upon what God is showing you, or nothing will happen. The successful operation of these gifts requires a cooperation between you and God. You do your part, and He does the rest. You do what you can do, and He does all the things you cannot do.

But don't just sit around wishing you had more faith. Get up and put to work the faith you already have, and then you'll get more. Let your faith be a living and active faith, and it will also be a growing faith.

Old-fashioned Men and Women of Faith Knew How to Move the Hand of God

Old-fashioned men and women of faith knew how to move the hand of God. They would get on the radio and announce, "Bring all the sick to the crusade tonight, and God will heal them." By doing this, they were exercising their faith, putting it into action. They were doing what they could, and then it was up to God to do the rest. The result was that He worked for them in amazing ways. God cannot fail us when we demonstrate living and active faith.

Some are carried away with enthusiasm and wonder why God doesn't honor their words. It may be because what they're saying isn't based on God's will, or His Word, but on what that person wants to see done. Enthusiasm can be totally carnal, but faith is always spiritual.

As we noted earlier, faith doesn't operate in the natural realm. You can wish for something all you want, but it won't happen as long as you're in the realm of the natural. This is the reason it's necessary for us to live in the realm of the Spirit, the realm of faith, and to be around people who are talking faith and walking faith.

Today, God is still looking for a people of increased faith. So take off all the attached strings, remove all the hindrances, and let Him work for you. Forget every limitation, and allow God to bless you and bless you, and bless you, and bless you some more—as He desires to do.

If you are sure you can't do something, then you won't. But if you are sure that He can, then He will.

Faith Upsets the Enemy

The enemy will get very upset when you start moving in faith, and he'll do everything in his power to stop you. But if you're willing to make a move, God will help you. You don't need a gigantic measure of faith to begin. Just use what you have, and it will grow. Your existing faith will move you into new areas of operation in God and will produce that which you need.

If you continue to minister in the same realms in which you've always moved, you'll never see anything greater done for God. But if you'll take the initiative, step over the barriers that have stood in your way, and begin to lay claim to the promises of the Lord, you'll begin to see His hand outstretched in a new way.

Living and Active Faith Raises You to a New Level

Once, when my sister Ruth and I arrived in New York to minister in a church there, we were met at the airport by a young man we knew, and he took us in a lovely automobile to the place where the service was being held. On the way to the church, he told me that he was planning to travel with us that fall to Israel. "What happened to you?" I asked. "This doesn't seem like the brother I used to know."

"No," he agreed. "I was in one of Brother R. W. Schambach's meetings, and God got hold of me. I decided to stop letting the devil push me around and to take what God was offering me. And it turned my life around." That fall both the man and his wife traveled with us to the Holy Land. His faith had come alive, he made a move, and God was there to meet him.

Our God is faithful. He never fails us, and He never disappoints us. We will always have victory when we move in faith.

What Simple Words!

I thank God for the simple words of James that make us to know that we must act on our faith. If we produce no works, our faith is dead, for it's only when we take steps of obedience that our faith comes alive.

So, if someone else can travel for God, then you, too, can travel for God. If someone else can believe God for a better car, then you, too, can believe Him for a better car. But you need to take some steps of faith. If God has told you to travel, start getting your travel documents in order. If He has promised you a new automobile, start getting your learner's permit. If God has promised you a new home, start looking for it. Let faith arise in your heart, and when that faith proves to be alive and active, you'll see God moving on your behalf. It's time to start *LIVING BY FAITH.*

Chapter 12

"Now" Faith

Now faith is the substance of things hoped for, the evidence of things not seen.

Hebrews 11:1

Every one of us needs a "now" faith, a faith that takes things that might be for the future and pulls them into the present. Stop believing for next month and next year, and start believing for NOW. Say, "Yes, God, I believe You will do it, and I believe You will do it NOW."

Don't Be Satisfied with Life as It Now Is

If you're satisfied with your situation and are willing to put up with it for the rest of your life, then you'll have to put up with it for the rest of your life. Your faith will produce no change. But when you get to the place that you're tired of being a doormat, tired of being used, tired of being walked on, tired of the situation continuing for so long without change, then the hand of God will be moved on your behalf. If you're ready for a change and you want that change, regardless of the price you have to pay, and you put your foot down and say, "Devil, this far and no farther; you have done all you're going to do to me," then you'll see God begin to work in an unusual way in your life. The change will come because you've made up your mind to see it NOW. You've had enough, and you simply won't put up with any more.

"Now" Faith Heals Tumors

One of the first nights of my tent meetings in Greenville, North Carolina, in 1978, a nineteen-year-old girl came into the meeting who had a tumor the size of a pear on her chest. "Does it hurt?" I asked.

She said, "No."

"Does it bother you?" I asked.

"No, but I am tired of having it," she said. "I've had it far too long."

"Well," I told her, "you're in the right place, and God's going to remove it."

She came back later in the crusade and testified that the growth was totally gone. If she had been satisfied to keep that thing, she would still have it. But when she got tired of it and wanted it gone, God did the miracle. Her faith was for NOW. I've seen it happen that way again and again. It's your "now" faith that moves the hand of God.

Cry Out, "God, It's Mine and It's Mine Now!"

If you think you could never have something, then you'll almost certainly never have it. But if you cry out, "God, it's mine, it's mine, because of Your Word, it's mine," you'll have it. And if you believe for it now, then you'll get it now. Let God know that you want it and that you want it now, and you'll have it.

Are you hoping for something? If so, then you need NOW faith to receive it. Don't believe that it will happen tomorrow. Believe that it will happen NOW. You need it NOW, and the Lord is willing to give it to you NOW if you will only exercise NOW faith.

LIVING BY FAITH

Our Lord has declared:

> *And it shall come to pass, that before they call, I will answer; and while they are yet speaking, I will hear.* Isaiah 65:24

The miracle you need may be waiting for you. If you're believing for it, God will do it, and He'll do it NOW. Friend, it's time to start *LIVING BY FAITH.*

Chapter 13

Walking Faith and Sleeping Faith

And Peter answered him and said, Lord, if it be thou, bid me come unto thee on the water. And he said, Come.   Matthew 14:28-29

Peter had faith to step out over the side of the boat and walk on the water. All he needed was to hear the voice of Jesus.

The answer of Jesus was simple. No reproach! No harangue! Simply, *"Come."* He welcomes faith that's ready to walk on water, and He honors it.

Jesus Didn't Have to Explain

Jesus didn't explain just how Peter was to walk on the water, and He gave no assurances that He would make the water as hard as concrete or that He would hold Peter up to keep him from sinking. He just said, *"Come."* But that was enough. Why? Because you can trust Jesus. You can rely on His word. You can leap over the side and walk toward Him—simply because He has spoken. You need no other reason, no other motivation. *Come*. That's enough.

God's Word will never fail you. It will sustain you, it will hold you up, it will keep you moving forward, and it will bring you safely to your destination. That word *"come"* changes everything, and when you hear it, suddenly you can walk on water.

Don't Wait for Anything Else

You don't need to have everything that God says in writing. You don't need to analyze it twenty-five different ways and get fifteen confirmations for it. When He says, *"Come,"* then just leap over the side of the boat and start walking. Do it by faith, and He will do the rest.

By the time you get that fifteenth confirmation, it may be too late. The opportunity will have passed, and the door will, no doubt, be closed to you. Move now. Act on the word of the Lord. *Come!* Have faith that walks on water.

Have Sleeping Faith

He giveth his beloved sleep.   Psalm 127:2

Daniel had enough faith to go to sleep when hungry lions were all about him in that famous lions' den. That means a lot. When you can rest in peace while all the world around you seems to be going wrong, that's a demonstration of your confidence in God and His ability to protect and keep you.

You don't need to pace the floor. You don't need to go over everything a hundred times in your mind. Go to bed and relax, and leave everything in God's hands. Sleep in peace by faith.

Counting sheep doesn't always work. You might count sheep for a long time, all night sometimes. Warm milk doesn't always do the trick. Rest in God's love.

Just say, "Holy Ghost, I trust You. Put me to sleep." It works for me every single time.

It doesn't matter how many problems you have. It doesn't matter how severe the pressures of the

149

moment are. You can rest in peace when you have faith in God.

Some people can't even sleep in the comfort of their own beds, but Daniel slept in the lions' den. You can have faith in the midst of adversity and sleep the sleep of the righteous.

God surely loves me, for I can sleep anywhere. I sleep on airplanes or while I'm riding along in a car. I can sleep on the floor or on a hard bed. I can sleep anywhere. I know that the angels of God are camped round about me and that I have nothing to worry about. So I drift off to sleep effortlessly.

Let's have walking faith and let's have sleeping faith. Refuse to dwell on all the problems at hand. Instead, dwell on the fact that God is able to bring us through every problem in great victory. It's time to start *LIVING BY FAITH.*

Chapter 14

Multiplying Faith

Then he took the five loaves and the two fishes, and looking up to heaven, he blessed them, and brake, and gave to the disciples to set before the multitude. And they did eat, and were all filled: and there was taken up of fragments that remained to them twelve baskets. Luke 9:16-17

There is a lad here, which hath five barley loaves, and two small fishes: but what are they among so many? John 6:9

God wants to give you multiplying faith, faith that He will put His hand on the little you have and do a miracle to make it much. When it happens, everyone is amazed—even those of us to whom it happens.

My parents were people of multiplying faith.

They were constantly believing God to multiply the gasoline in their tank, to multiply their church offerings so that they would be large enough to pay all the bills, to multiply their sleep so that they could get enough rest in fewer hours. And God did this for them—time and time again.

The Fruits of Multiplying Faith

We've had multiplying faith for our camp in Ashland. The more we give away, the more God gives us. We receive donations from hospitals, hotels, and motels of beds and other furniture, carpets, and kitchen equipment; and theaters give us theater seats. We can't possibly use it all, so we give many of the things we receive to other ministries, and the Lord continues to give us more. He never fails. When we believe for our little to be blessed, He multiplies it. It's wonderful to see our faith producing truckloads of materials for His Kingdom.

Let us stretch beyond that for which we have believed in the past, so that we can reach forth to the greater things. Let your faith be increased and turned into multiplying faith.

Reject Doubt

Never let doubt cross your mind, and if doubt does creep in, rebuke it. Chase it away. Put your foot down. Doubt, if it is allowed to linger, will destroy your faith and destroy you with it.

Don't let someone sit in your house and talk fear, doubt, and unbelief. You can't afford to allow it. It's too dangerous. It is too contagious.

"Suppose God doesn't do this."

"God can't do that."

"What will you do if He doesn't respond?"

You may not think this negative talk is affecting you at all, but by the time the person saying these things leaves your house, you've been contaminated.

Let the skeptics rave, and let the scorners mock, but you must keep your victory in the midst of it all.

Doubters Chided
the Donor of the Camp Land

When Sister Ruth Brown gave the original fifteen acres of land for the camp in Ashland, her friends told her she was foolish for doing it. "They'll never do anything with that land," they said. "You've just thrown your money away."

When the first building was started on the campground, she told her friends about it, and they assured her that it would be the last, and that nothing more would come of it. Then a second building was added, and so forth, until the camp became a place of spiritual watering for the nations. So don't worry about what other people say. You obey God, and He'll give you multiplying faith.

Skeptics Will Try to Run Your Life

The doubters and skeptics who want to sit on the sidelines and do nothing will try to tell you how you should run your life, but please don't listen to them. Don't listen to unsuccessful people. Don't listen to the "do-nothings" of this world. Just keep on traveling. Just keep on giving. Just keep on doing what God has told you to do. Perhaps one day all those other people who say it can't be done will realize that they're the ones who have missed out because they failed to let their faith go to believe for the impossible. I encourage you to have multiplying faith. Friend, it's time to start *Living by Faith.*

Chapter 15

Unwavering Faith

But let him ask in faith, nothing wavering. For he that wavereth is like a wave of the sea driven with the wind and tossed. For let not that man think that he shall receive any thing of the Lord.

James 1:6-7

The secret of receiving the miracle you need is to have an unwavering faith. This means that you move ahead by faith and never let doubt cross your mind.

Unbelief Is a Powerful Seed

Unbelief is such a powerful seed that if you allow it to take root, it will destroy your life. So don't give place to it. Talk faith, think faith, and act faith. Move doubt aside.

This requires that you never give up. If you've already prayed for something a thousand times and you still haven't gotten your answer, it's time to pray prayer number 1,001. Your miracle is coming. So don't ever give up.

If someone has prayed for you already twenty-five times, get prayed for again. It's never too late in God. He is about to work for you. Keep believing. Keep insisting. Keep knocking on the door of opportunity, and keep looking up. It's unwavering faith that produces results.

Don't Stay Where Doubt Rules

Don't stay around people who sow doubt and try to destroy faith. Separate yourself from them. You must not let anything or anyone hinder your faith. Avoid those who are unwilling to submit themselves to the teachings of the Word of God and who ridicule its importance. They can do you no good.

If that's the kind of people you're around, then find better company. Find an atmosphere where your faith can grow and flourish, and your life will be so much different.

Two Families Needed Healing

Many years ago two families from another Pentecostal church in Richmond began attending our services.

They were drawn to us because of the miracles of healing God was doing in our church. Every member of those two families had some serious physical ailment. They were all sick. One after the other was admitted to the hospital, and one after the other required surgery.

Their preacher had prayed, their church had prayed, and they had prayed, and yet their physical conditions did not improve. Finally, in desperation, they decided to find a church where faith was preached so that they could lay hold of it and escape the ills that were constantly tormenting them. In their case, it was either faith or death.

Once they began coming to our church and feeding from the diet of faith my parents constantly dished up, their physical problems were conquered, and they rejoiced in good health.

Let the Word Be "Mixed with Faith"

Some people can even have the Gospel, and yet it doesn't seem to do them any good. Why is that? It's because the Gospel they know is not *"mixed with faith"*:

> *For unto us was the gospel preached, as well as unto them: but the word preached did not profit them, not being mixed with faith in them that heard it.* Hebrews 4:2

Fear and unbelief are the subjects of far too many pulpits. It's time to preach unwavering faith. This has been the hallmark of our ministry now for many years, and it had its roots in my father's persistent faith.

When he was with a large Pentecostal organization, they often held three-day conventions. In many of those meetings, there would be three speakers. One would speak on the Holy Ghost baptism, a second would preach on the second coming of Christ, and a third would preach on faith and healing and then pray for the sick. Dad was often called on to preach about faith and healing and to pray for the sick, because God used him to bring healing to many.

In time, it became a joke in the conference that when Dad's turn came to preach on the second coming, he would end up preaching on faith. When he started out preaching on the baptism of the Holy Ghost, he would end up preaching on faith. The other preachers came to the conclusion that he couldn't preach anything else.

This bothered my father and he decided one day, "I will show them that I know how to preach on other subjects," so he varied his messages in the coming days and weeks. But something happened. He noticed that when he prayed for the sick, he wasn't getting the same results. He would pray a second and a third time for some, wondering why his prayers were not as effective as before.

It bothered him so much that he complained to God. "God, I don't understand. You've always honored my faith. Every time I've prayed for the sick, You've been there to respond and to bring the miracle. Now, I'm preaching harder than I've ever preached, and I'm praying two and three times for each sick person, but I'm still not satisfied with the result. What's wrong?"

The Lord answered him, "You're not feeding the people as before." That day he decided to forget what men said about his preaching and to be willing to be branded as a one-subject preacher if it meant seeing the hand of God move in his life and ministry. He tried it, going back to what seemed natural to him, building up the people's faith before praying for them, and soon the miracles returned to his ministry with the same intensity. You need faith, you need more faith, you need strong faith, and you need unwavering faith.

Things That Destroy Faith

A doctor's diagnosis can destroy some people's faith in just a few moments' time. "The cancer has spread to her brain. She's too far gone." With those few words, their faith vanishes. Just that quickly faith can be destroyed.

But God didn't say, "She's too far gone." He taught us in His Word to say:

> *I can do all things through Christ which strengtheneth me.* Philippians 4:13

Meditate on these powerful words a moment:

I CAN!
I CAN DO!
I CAN DO ALL!
I CAN DO ALL THINGS!
I CAN DO ALL THINGS THROUGH CHRIST!
I CAN DO ALL THINGS THROUGH CHRIST WHICH STRENGTHENETH ME!

God said:

> *Nothing shall be impossible unto you.*
> Matthew 17:20

Hold fast to those promises and never let them go. Have unwavering faith.

The World Is Flooded with Cynicism and Skepticism

With the flood of cynicism and skepticism sweeping the world today, is it any wonder Jesus asked the question:

When the Son of man cometh, shall he find faith on the earth?   Luke 18:8

Hold on, dear one! Hold on! Don't let go! God is still on the throne, and He's still performing miracles for those who demonstrate unwavering faith.

God Cannot Honor Doubt

If you were filled with doubt, fear and unbelief, if you were bound by your circumstances, and God came and worked for you, He would be honoring doubt, fear, and unbelief. But these are the things He hates most, the things that are most offensive to Him. So He can't do it. As much as He loves you, He can't do it. As much as He would like to, He can't do it. As much as He feels your burdens and longs to lift them all, He can't do it.

He simply cannot honor that which is contrary to faith, for He has bound Himself to it. He has said:

Whatsoever is not of faith is sin.
Romans 14:23

Fear is not of God; it is the enemy of God. Doubt is not of God; it is the enemy of God. Unbelief is not of God; it is contrary to God. Therefore He cannot honor it. What He honors is unwavering faith.

If you've been around people who are constantly talking doubt and unbelief, you know that it can affect everyone around them very quickly. Get away from those people. They'll not only give you a headache; they'll destroy your soul—if you stay around them long enough.

I don't like to be around that. I don't need that. I need an atmosphere that is positive and forward looking. I don't need to hear all the "but-what-ifs." These people don't believe that God can do anything, and I believe just the opposite—that He can do anything and everything. So, we're incompatible. I must have unwavering faith. It's time to start *LIVING BY FAITH.*

Chapter 16

Remembering Faith

Remember the word that I said unto you.

John 15:20

When God gives us a promise, we must remember it. Satan will do everything in his power to make us forget it, but God calls upon us to *"remember."*

Remembering Words of Prophecy

When I receive a personal prophecy, I have someone type it up for me from the tape, and then I keep the printout handy somewhere—either on my desk or in my Bible. I want to remember what God has promised me, and I want to meditate on what He has said He will do for me.

In the difficult times, I don't want to have my faith dragged down by the impossibilities and the darkness of the moment. I want to remember

163

what God said was coming. And, in remembering, I am blessed.

In prison in Egypt, Joseph remembered the dreams God had given him in which his brothers were bowing down to him. That remembrance sustained him through hard times and eventually brought him to power.

Now Is the Time to Remember

When Abraham appeared to the rich man who died and was in torment in the flames of Hell, he called upon him to *"remember"*:

> *But Abraham said, Son, remember that thou in thy lifetime receivedst thy good things, and likewise Lazarus evil things: but now he is comforted, and thou art tormented.*
>
> Luke 16:25

But that was a bad time to be remembering. It's now, while we still have breath, while we still have time, while God can still do something for us, that we need to remember.

Abraham made the rich man remember the banquets in which he *"fared sumptuously,"* while the beggar at his gate settled for whatever leftovers were thrown his way. When rich people get to Hell, they'll remember how they used to let the water run because it was so cheap. Like this rich man, they'll long for just one drop of that water to moisten their tongues, but it will not be found.

They'll remember how they had no time for others, now that they're crying out for someone, anyone, to help *them*. Remembering, for them, will be a double torture, and it will be too late to do them any good.

But you and I still have time. We can still escape the torments of Hell. We can remember now. We must allow the Holy Ghost to make such an impression upon our souls that nothing will be able to move us aside from God's ways.

One day, when Jesus was preaching, He declared:

Remember Lot's wife.   Luke 17:32

What a simple message! Remember! Have remembering faith! When you remember, it changes everything.

Remembering the Past Gives Us Faith for the Future

The disciples of Jesus sometimes needed to be

reminded of what God had already done in their lives so that they could have faith for the future:

> *Do ye not yet understand, neither remember the five loaves of the five thousand, and how many baskets ye took up?*   Matthew 16:9

Jesus also challenged the disciples to keep remembering when He would no longer be with them:

> *But these things have I told you, that when the time shall come, ye may remember that I told you of them. And these things I said not unto you at the beginning, because I was with you.*   John 16:4

The early apostles challenged the members of the Church to remember:

> *I have showed you all things, how that so labouring ye ought to support the weak, and to REMEMBER the words of the Lord Jesus, how he said, It is more blessed to give than to receive.*   Acts 20:35

REMEMBERING FAITH

Paul praised the Corinthians for remembering:

Now I praise you, brethren, that ye remember me in all things, and keep the ordinances, as I delivered them to you.

1 Corinthians 11:2

They hadn't always remembered, for at one point he sent Timothy to them to help them remember:

For this cause have I sent unto you Timotheus, who is my beloved son, and faithful in the Lord, who shall bring you into remembrance of my ways which be in Christ, as I teach every where in every church. 1 Corinthians 4:17

Timothy himself needed some reminding at another time in his life:

Wherefore I put thee in remembrance that thou stir up the gift of God, which is in thee by the putting on of my hands.

2 Timothy 1:6

Taking Communion Is
an Act of Remembering

The communion table was instituted by the Lord as a remembrance of what He has done for us:

> *And he took bread, and gave thanks, and brake it, and gave unto them, saying, This is my body which is given for you: this do in remembrance of me.* Luke 22:19

Part of the work of the Holy Ghost is to *"bring to* [our] *remembrance"* the things the Lord has spoken to us:

> *But the Comforter, which is the Holy Ghost, whom the Father will send in my name, he shall teach you all things, and bring all things to your remembrance, whatsoever I have said unto you.* John 14:26

Remembering is powerful, and forgetting is dangerous to our spiritual health. Have remembering faith. It's time to start *LIVING BY FAITH*. ⤶

Chapter 17

Joining Faith to Faith

When Jesus saw THEIR faith, he said unto the sick of the palsy, Son, thy sins be forgiven thee.   Mark 2:5

The faith of any one person is powerful, but when we can join faith to faith, much more can be accomplished.

I Joined My Faith to My Parents' Faith

When I got saved in 1963, we were still worshiping in a small tabernacle on the campground. We also had a small chapel, a small dining hall, a snack bar, and two small cabins. When those two cabins, usually reserved for camp speakers, were filled, everyone else slept in tents or in my parents' house.

When I added my faith to my parents' faith, something began to happen. I probably can't take much of the credit. Mother always said, "You and your dad make all the bills, and I have to pray in the money to cover them." Whatever the case, something began to happen, and we began to add many new and wonderful facilities to the camp.

When we join faith to faith, marvelous things can be accomplished for the Kingdom of God. Therefore, in every ministry, we must stop depending on the faith of a single person, and everyone must get involved. As we join faith to faith, great things can result.

Stand with Others of Like Precious Faith

Peter was unwilling to stand with Jesus when He was taken into the house of Caiaphas, and he had to repent for it later. He swore that he didn't even know Jesus, and that is typical of how we sometimes treat our brothers when they're in a difficult position.

One of the reasons my father was always in hot water with the leadership of a denomination he belonged to for some years was that he would stand by anyone he felt was right. When he saw that someone was being "railroaded," he couldn't sit still for it. He had to take a stand for them, and he had to do it publicly. He simply couldn't deny his brothers for any reason.

When others didn't want to identify with some controversial ministry figure, Dad was right there by their side. When revival came to Richmond in the late 1940s, many of the local ministers didn't want to put their names on the line for the people God used to bring the revival, mainly because the principal preacher was a fourteen-year-old boy. But my parents stuck their necks out and sponsored the meetings, signing for all the rentals, the advertising, etc., so that the revival meetings could go forward, and God blessed them because of it.

Michal Despised David

When David was leading the Ark into the capital city, he felt the glory of God so powerfully that he began to leap and dance. His wife, instead of joining her husband in his rejoicing, despised him for what he was doing. He was the king, after all, and should act like a king. Michal was ashamed of

David and wanted no part of what he was doing, but if she had felt what David was feeling, she would have joined him in his rejoicing.

The Scriptures declare that if we are ashamed of Jesus, He will be ashamed of us. And, in the same way, if we're ashamed of our brothers who love the Lord and are working for Him, the results will be the same. Join faith to faith. Stand side by side. Work together for the glory of the Kingdom of God.

Stand with Men and Women of Faith

Because we know what it is to have others turn on us and leave us standing alone, we should always be ready to stand with a brother or sister and take their part when the world (or the carnal church) comes against them. Don't believe every bad report you hear about others, and be willing to identify with a brother or sister in their moment of attack. Then, in your hour of need, there will be someone willing to stand with you.

A fellow minister called me one day to say that someone was trying to split his church. He wanted me to help him by coming to preach to his people. It was definitely not a convenient time, and yet I felt compelled to cancel what I was doing and fly to his city to preach. After I had finished, I would have to leave very early the next morning to get back home to my responsibilities there, but I could not say no to him. I had to help him take a stand.

Stand side by side and shoulder to shoulder with those who are of like precious faith and of like spirit, and do it whether it's convenient or not. They don't need you when the sun is shining and everything is going well. But when they need you, they need you.

I wouldn't walk across the street to stand for someone who's compromising with the world and lowering their standards. But I am willing to make a great sacrifice to stand up for those who are trying to do the right thing.

Speak an Encouraging Word

I once loaned one of my gospel tents to three businessmen who were led to conduct an evangelistic crusade. It was a lovely tent with four sections, each of them thirty feet long and sixty feet wide, so the total size of the tent was one hundred and twenty feet by sixty feet. Every one of those sections was about to be torn to shreds in a wind storm.

Only a few days after their meeting began, one of the men called me, and said, "Brother Heflin, you'd better sit down. I have something to tell you."

"What's the matter?" I asked.

He said, "You won't believe what happened. A storm just tore the tent up."

He was so sad, for it was his first venture of faith, and the meeting was only about three days old. But he felt even worse because it was my tent and they had borrowed it.

But as he told me what had happened, I knew what had to be done. "Listen, brother," I told him, "I'll bring some men there tomorrow, and we'll take the torn tent down, but I have another tent, an older one. We'll bring it with us, and we'll put it up for you, so your meetings can continue." When those simple words were spoken, I could feel his spirit rise on the other end of the line. The terrible heaviness that had been hanging over him began to lift.

I took some men and went there the next day. We took the other tent down and put the older one up in its place. In less than four hours, the switch was complete, and we were on our way back home. From that moment on, those meetings accelerated, and by the closing night, they had a lovely crowd.

174

The brothers who had done the preaching were on cloud nine. If I hadn't been about to have my own meeting in North Carolina, they said, they would have wanted to continue preaching in the tent.

My encouragement had changed everything for them. One minute they had been completely down, and the next minute they were up again.

Jesus Came to Comfort the Disciples

The day Jesus was crucified, the entire city was in an uproar. It was an uproar that lasted for some time, and it drove the disciples to lock themselves into private rooms for fear of what might be done to them just for being His disciples, just for being His friends. When Jesus decided to appear to them, He had to go through locked doors to do it.

And He'll be there for you, too. God knows how to strengthen your faith. Each of us should just refuse to allow the devil to get us down. Jesus is alive and He's always with us. What do we have to fear? It doesn't matter how dark your situation might seem. There's victory and deliverance in Jesus Christ. He's a way-making God. Have faith in Him. It's time to start *Living by Faith*.

175

Part V

Living by Faith

Chapter 18

What Does It Mean to Live by Faith?

Through faith we understand.
Hebrews 11:3

By faith Abel offered unto God.
Hebrews 11:4

By faith Enoch was translated.
Hebrews 11:5

By faith Noah ... prepared an ark.
Hebrews 11:7

By faith Abraham ... obeyed.
Hebrews 11:8

By faith he [Abraham] *sojourned in the land of promise.*
Hebrews 11:9

LIVING BY FAITH

Through faith ... Sarah ... received strength to conceive.   Hebrews 11:11

By faith Abraham ... offered up Isaac.
                                    Hebrews 11:17

By faith Isaac blessed Jacob and Esau concerning things to come.   Hebrews 11:20

By faith Jacob ... blessed both the sons of Joseph; and worshipped.   Hebrews 11:21

By faith Joseph ... made mention of the departing of the children of Israel; and gave commandment concerning his bones.
                                    Hebrews 11:22

By faith Moses ... was hid three months of his parents.   Hebrews 11:23

By faith Moses ... refused to be called the son of Pharaoh's daughter.   Hebrews 11:24

By faith he [Moses] forsook Egypt.
                                    Hebrews 11:27

180

WHAT DOES IT MEAN TO LIVE BY FAITH?

Through faith he [Moses] *kept the passover .*
Hebrews 11:28

By faith they [the children of Israel] *passed through the Red sea.*   Hebrews 11:29

By faith the walls of Jericho fell down.
Hebrews 11:30

By faith the harlot Rahab perished not.
Hebrews 11:31

And what shall I more say? for the time would fail me to tell of Gedeon, and of Barak, and of Samson, and of Jephthae; of David also, and Samuel, and of the prophets.   Hebrews 11:32

It was all done *"by faith,"* or *"through faith,"* and that's because everything begins with faith in God. Salvation begins *"by faith."* Healing begins *"by faith."* Holy Ghost power begins *"by faith."* Ministries begin *"by faith."* Missions begin *"by faith."* Without faith, we are nothing, we have nothing, and we can do nothing. It is faith that connects us to the Source of all supply.

LIVING BY FAITH

If you don't do something *"by faith,"* it won't be done. If you don't walk *"by faith,"* you won't walk successfully, and if you don't act *"by faith,"* your actions won't be blessed.

There were Abel, Enoch, Noah, Abraham, Sarah, Isaac, Jacob, Joseph, Moses, the children of Israel, Rahab, Gideon, Barak, Samson, Jephthah, David, Samuel, the other prophets, and an unnamed woman ... and now add your name to the list. God is calling you today to live by faith, to act by faith, to walk by faith. And it's time to take the first steps.

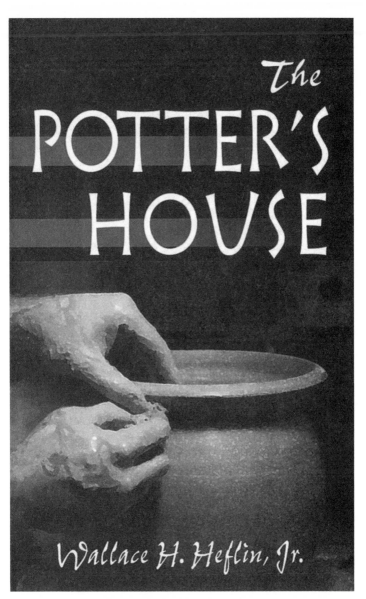

The Potter's House 978-1-884369-61-2

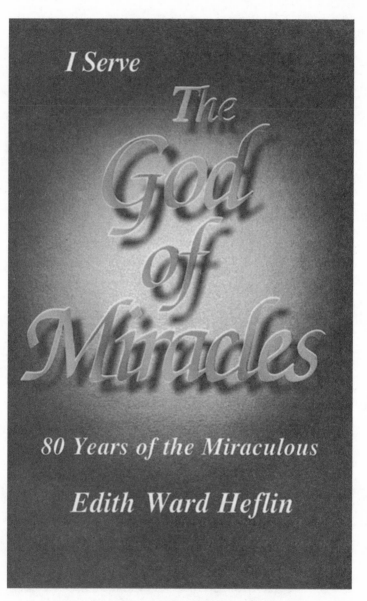

God of Miracles 1-56043-043-5

HIGH and LIFTED UP

How Seeing Jesus Propelled
a Sharecropper's Daughter
Into Worldwide Evangelism

Jane Lowder

High and Lifted Up 978-1-58158-050-1

Revelation Glory 978-1-58158-010-5

The BESTSELLING:

GLORY

by
Ruth Ward Heflin

What is Glory?

- *It is the realm of eternity.*
- *It is the revelation of the presence of God.*
- *He is the glory! As air is the atmosphere of the Earth, so glory is the atmosphere of Heaven.*

Praise ... until the spirit of worship comes. Worship ... until the glory comes. Then ... stand in the glory. If you can capture the basic principles of praise, worship and glory which are outlined in this book — so simple that we often miss them — you can have anything else you want in God.

ISBN 1-884369-00-6

Ask for it at your favorite bookstore or from:
Calvary Books
11352 Heflin Lane
Ashland, VA 23005
(804) 798-7756
www.calvarycampground.org

Other books
by
Rev. Wallace H. Heflin, Jr.

A Pocket Full of Miracles   0-914903-23-3

Bride, The   1-884369-10-3

Jacob and Esau   1-884369-01-4

The Potter's House   1-884369-61-8

Power In Your Hand   1-884369-60-X

Power In Your Hand *(Spanish Edition)*
                            1-884369-04-9

Ask for them at your favorite bookstore or from:
Calvary Books
11352 Heflin Lane
Ashland, VA 23005
(804) 798-7756
www.calvarycampground.org

Books by Dr. William A. Ward

Miracles That I Have Seen	1-884369-79-0
God Can Turn Things Around	1-56043-014-1
On the Edge of Time	0-91490347-0
Get Off the Ash Heap	1-884369-20-0
Christian Cybernetics	1-884369-19-7
How to Be Successful	

Ask for them at your favorite bookstore or from:

Calvary Books
11352 Heflin Lane
Ashland, VA 23005
(804) 798-7756
www.calvarycampground.org

Calvary Pentecostal Tabernacle

11352 Heflin Lane
Ashland, VA 23005

Tel. (804) 798-7756
Fax. (804) 752-2163
www.calvarycampground.org

Summer Campmeetings

End of June through August

With two great services daily, 11 A.M. & 7:30 P.M.

Winter Campmeetings

First Friday of February through the end of February

Revival Meetings

Each Friday night, Saturday morning, Saturday night and
Sunday night revival meeting

*Ministry tapes and song tapes are also available upon
request.*

info@calvarycampground.org